T0312051

Cambridge Elements ☰

Elements in Contentious Politics
edited by
David S. Meyer
University of California, Irvine
Suzanne Staggenborg
University of Pittsburgh

THE PHANTOM AT THE OPERA

Social Movements and Institutional Politics

Sidney Tarrow
Cornell University, New York

CAMBRIDGE
UNIVERSITY PRESS

CAMBRIDGE
UNIVERSITY PRESS

University Printing House, Cambridge CB2 8BS, United Kingdom

One Liberty Plaza, 20th Floor, New York, NY 10006, USA

477 Williamstown Road, Port Melbourne, VIC 3207, Australia

314–321, 3rd Floor, Plot 3, Splendor Forum, Jasola District Centre,
New Delhi – 110025, India

103 Penang Road, #05–06/07, Visioncrest Commercial, Singapore 238467

Cambridge University Press is part of the University of Cambridge.

It furthers the University's mission by disseminating knowledge in the pursuit of
education, learning, and research at the highest international levels of excellence.

www.cambridge.org
Information on this title: www.cambridge.org/9781009044516
DOI: 10.1017/9781009043731

First published 2021

A catalogue record for this publication is available from the British Library.

ISBN 978-1-009-04451-6 Paperback
ISSN 2633-3570 (online)
ISSN 2633-3562 (print)

The Phantom at The Opera

Social Movements and Institutional Politics

Elements in Contentious Politics

DOI: 10.1017/9781009043731
First published online: December 2021

Sidney Tarrow
Cornell University, New York

Author for correspondence: Sidney Tarrow, sgt2@cornell.edu

Abstract: Movements and parties have given rise to two largely separate specialties in the social sciences. This Element is an effort to link the two literatures, using evidence from American political development. It identifies five relational mechanisms governing movement/party relations: two of them short term, two intermediate term, and one long-term. It closes with a reflection on the role of movement/party relations in democratization and for democratic resilience.

Keywords: American political development, elections, hybrid movements, movement-parties, political parties, relatonal mechanisms, social movements.

ISBNs: 9781009044516 (PB), 9781009043731 (OC)
ISSNs: 2633-3570 (online), 2633-3562 (print)

Contents

Introduction   1

1 What Was Happening Here?   4

2 Moves Toward Fusion   7

3 Movement/Party Relations in Critical Junctures   19

4 Two Short-Term Linkage Mechanisms   23

5 Two Intermediate-Level Mechanisms   30

6 Movements, Parties, and Democracy   36

References   41

Introduction

On May 25, 2020, a black man named George Floyd was arrested outside a store in Minneapolis, where he had been suspected of trying to pass counterfeit money.[1] First seen on a cellphone video with his hands manacled, Floyd was recorded on the ground next to a police cruiser, with a policeman's knee pressed against his neck. When he complained that he could not breathe, the policeman, Derek Chauvin, told him to stop shouting, while three other police officers stood by and watched. Floyd died shortly after, and Chauvin was charged with third-degree murder by the Minneapolis District Attorney.[2]

As is now well known, building on outrage at other recent killings of black people, Floyd's murder led to a massive protest movement.[3] This was the largest wave of protest in the country's history, according to scholars interviewed by *The New York Times*. "I've never seen self-reports of protest participation that high for a specific issue over such a short period," said Neal Caren, editor of the prestigious academic journal, *Mobilization*.[4] The protest movement was black, white, small town, and big city, and rapidly spread across the country. It was "a demographic mix that is far more varied than anything we have seen in recent years," wrote Doug McAdam soon after. Indeed, writes McAdam, the mix is "far more diverse than anything we saw during the heyday of the mass Civil Rights Movement of the 1960s."[5]

Anger at the killing was amplified by the frustration that had bubbled up at the racial bigotry of President Donald Trump, beginning with his campaign claim that Mexico is "sending us rapists." Moreover, the Covid-19 pandemic and the ensuing lockdown of schools and businesses left thousands of young people suddenly and unexpectedly thrown into a state of precarity and hardship (Chen 2020:25). But probably the most fundamental source of the mass agitation was the Black Lives Matter (BLM) movement.

That movement had begun in July 2013, when George Zimmerman, who had killed a black teenager, Trayvon Martin, under cover of Florida's "Stand Your

---

[1] www.bbc.com/news/world-us-canada-52861726.

[2] www.nytimes.com/2020/05/29/us/derek-chauvin-criminal-complaint.html.

[3] Well worth reading is Larry Buchanan, Quoctrung Bui and Jugal K. Patelm "Black Lives Matter May be the Largest Movement in US History," *New York Times*, July 3, 2020. www.nytimes.com /interactive/2020/07/03/us/george-floyd-protests-crowd-size.html

[4] Compare this to the women's march following the inauguration of Donald Trump, when between three and five million people turned out. Erica Chenoweth and Jeffrey Pressman, "This is What We Learned by Counting the Women's Marches," *The Monkey Cage*, February 7, 2017. www .washingtonpost.com/news/monkey-cage/wp/2017/02/07/this-is-what-we-learned-by-counting-the-womens-marches/.

[5] Doug McAdam, "We've Never Seen Protests Like These Before," *Jacobin*, June 20, 2020. www .jacobinmag.com/2020/06/george-floyd-protests-black-lives-matter-riots-demonstrations.

Ground" law, was acquitted.[6] It became a national movement after the police killings of two other black men: Michael Brown in Ferguson, Missouri, and Eric Garner in New York City, both in 2014. From that point on, BLM became synonymous with black and minority rights. Although it was viewed initially with suspicion by many Whites, by June 2020 the movement had gained majority support from all major ethnic groups – including more than 60 percent of Whites.[7] As in past cycles of contention, it also had a lateral influence on other movements: on the young people's climate change movement that had exploded in the previous year;[8] on healthcare workers who added support for racial justice to their protests against the mismanagement of the pandemic;[9] and in more than eighty cities and counties that declared racism a "public health crisis.[10] It looks," remarked McAdam to the *Times*, that "We appear to be experiencing a social change tipping point – that is as rare in society as it is potentially consequential."[11]

Like the black urban movements of the 1960s, rage over Floyd's killing helped to trigger a movement/countermovement dynamic. White militants under a variety of labels organized wherever there were strong and visible BLM protests. They were soon supported by federal forces under Attorney General Bill Barr. In Portland, Oregon, in response to attacks on federal property, federal paramilitary forces were photographed bundling protesters into unmarked vans.[12] In Washington, DC, Trump's use of a church as a backdrop for a photo-op led to the brutalization of peaceful demonstrators by paramilitary police outside the White House.

The use of armed federal forces to repress peaceful protesters in her city did not sit well with Muriel Bowser, mayor of the District of Columbia. In a direct challenge to the president, she condemned the uninvited presence of federal forces on the streets of her city and renamed Lafayette Square "Black Lives Matter Plaza."[13] Not to be outdone, when a group of BLM activists decided to paint the words "Black Lives Matter" in front of Trump Tower in New York

---

[6] www.usatoday.com/story/news/nation/2013/07/13/george-zimmerman-found-not-guilty
/2514163/.

[7] www.nytimes.com/2020/06/12/us/george-floyd-white-protesters.html.

[8] www.theguardian.com/us-news/2020/aug/03/young-climate-activists-rallies-us-elections-coronavirus?CMP=Share_iOSApp_Other.

[9] www.statnews.com/2020/06/16/doctors-protesting-racial-injustice/.

[10] www.vice.com/en_us/article/wxq4v5/more-than-80-cities-and-counties-have-now-declared-racism-a-public-health-crisis.

[11] Quoted in note no. 10.

[12] www.npr.org/2020/07/17/892277592/federal-officers-use-unmarked-vehicles-to-grab-protesters-in-portland.

[13] https://nationalpost.com/news/world/washington-emblazons-defiant-black-lives-matter-sign-near-white-house.

City, Mayor Bill de Blasio joined them, adopting the language of patriotism to applaud the protesters. "When we say 'Black Lives Matter'," he pronounced, "there is no more American statement, there is no more patriotic statement because there is no America without Black America."[14]

The impact of the protest wave was soon reflected in both political parties. Like Richard Nixon in 1968, Trump saw in the protests an opportunity to give a "law-and-order" framing to his lagging re-election campaign.[15] Trump and Barr accused Black Lives Matter of wanting to "tear down the system," trying to stoke fear among white voters by trying to redefine the movement as a radical leftist mob looking to sabotage the white, suburban lifestyle.[16]

There were also effects on the usually slow-to-change Democratic Party, where progressive black activists began to challenge aging members of the Congressional Black Caucus.[17] At its August 2020 national convention, the party focused heavily on racial justice.[18] Its ability to bring out the black and youth vote – in contrast to the unfortunate Hillary Clinton campaign four years earlier – helped Joe Biden and his mixed-race running mate, Kamala Harris, win the November election.

From protest to counterprotest to electoral politics, the sequence of events from George Floyd's murder in the spring of 2020 to Biden's victory in the fall constituted a critical juncture that turned American politics 180 degrees from its crisis under Donald Trump to its resilience six months later (Lieberman et al. 2021). Trump's refusal to accept the outcome of the election and his incitement of the assault on the Capitol on January 6, 2021, only heightened the tension in American society, especially when it turned out that much of the former president's base appeared to believe his misrepresentation of what appeared to be a clean and well-organized election. As late as April 2021, a majority of Republican voters continued to believe that the election had been stolen, a claim that was echoed by a number of high-ranking Republican members of Congress.[19] The Trump movement was the tail leading the Republican dog.

---

[14] www1.nyc.gov/office-of-the-mayor/news/508-20/transcript-mayor-de-blasio-helps-paint-new-black-lives-matter-mural-outside-trump-tower.

[15] www.cnn.com/2020/07/25/politics/trump-campaign-protest-federal-intervention/index.html.

[16] www.politico.com/news/2020/08/10/elections-republicans-black-lives-matterbacklash-389906.

[17] Aaron Ross Coleman, "Cori Bush's Victory Signals the Return of the Protester-Politician," *Vox*, August 8, 2020.

[18] https://thehill.com/homenews/campaign/511932-black-lives-matter-movement-to-play-elevated-role-at-convention. Compare the lineup at the party's 2016 convention when the mothers of black men killed by the police were the main reflection of its concern with racial injustice: www.latimes.com/politics/la-na-pol-democrats-black-lives-matter-20160727-snap-story.html.

[19] "Over Half of Republicans Believe Election Was Stolen from Trump: Poll," MSNBC, April 6, 2021. www.msnbc.com/morning-joe/watch/over-half-of-republicans-believe-election-was-stolenfrom-trump-poll-109731909987.

1 What Was Happening Here?

This was not the first time in American history that a movement/party linkage helped to transform American politics. From the Abolitionist/Republican linkage that supported the civil war and produced the Reconstruction Amendments, to the transformation of the agrarian movement into the Populist Party in the 1890s, to the impact of organized labor and civil rights on the Democrats in the 1930s and 1960s, to the infusion of the Christian Right into the Republican Party in the 1970s and 1980s, social movements have frequently been key "anchors" in the transformation of the party system (Schlozman 2015; Tarrow 2021). Often, they pushed parties and presidents to make profound changes in American institutions (Milkis and Tichenor 2019); sometimes, they brought about major changes in the political economy (Schickler 2016); more rarely, they were the pivots between democratization and de-democratization.

The events from the spring of 2020 through the presidential election in November of that year led supporters of American democracy to heave a sigh of relief (Mettler and Lieberman 2020). They also drew the attention of political scientists and sociologists. But while students of social movements focused on the phenomenology, the origins, and the discourse of the protesters (Chen 2020; McAdam 2020), political scientists were more interested in the response of the voters and in the effects of the protest wave on the coming election. With the exception of figures such as Caren and McAdam, they cordially ignored each others' contributions.

In this section, I will examine the reasons for this strangely bifurcated reaction in two fields that share theoretical and empirical interests in contentious politics. Then, in Section 2, I will highlight three recent efforts to "fuse" research on movements, parties, and elections. In Section 3, I will identify the mechanisms that bring movement and party perspectives together during critical junctures. In Sections 4 and 5, I will briefly illustrate two short-term mechanisms and two intermediate ones, drawing on a number of historical cases of movement/party interaction. The Element will conclude with some reflections on a fifth potential mechanism: the long-term impact of party/movement relations on American democracy. This will take us back to the travails of American democracy under the Trump administration and to the events of 2020.

Movement and Party Scholarship: A Curious Lacuna

Both social movement research and studies of political parties and elections are well-developed traditions in the United States. But until quite recently, and unlike the situation in Europe (Kriesi et al. 2020) or Latin America (Donoso and von Bülow 2017), disciplinary and methodological barriers hampered a synthesis between the two fields. While the study of parties has been seen as the proper province of political scientists, research on movements has largely been left to sociologists (Gamson 1990; Goldstone 2003; McAdam and Tarrow 2010). As Jack Goldstone observed in the introduction to his edited book, *States, Parties and Social Movements*:

> There has been a persistent tendency to see this interaction [between movements and the state] as distinct from normal institutionalized politics occurring through voting, lobbying, political parties, legislatures, courts, and elected leaders. (2003:1)

More recently, coming from the European tradition, Donatella della Porta and her collaborators complained that

> research on parties moved away from concerns with the relations between parties and society ... and social movement studies mainly framed them as a social phenomenon whose political aspects had to be located outside of the political institutions. (della Porta et al. 2017:3).

Although "the party in the electorate" was one of the three main legs of American party scholarship in the past (Key 1955), in recent decades the field has moved away from Key's focus on links between parties and society and toward the actions of elites and interest groups. This was in part the result of the influence of the methodological and theoretical individualism that became fashionable between the 1960s and the 1990s (Downs 1957; Aldrich 1995). That ontological shift moved the focus from parties as organizations (for example, see Mayhew 1986) to parties as majority-seeking office holders. John Aldrich, who best exemplified the approach, argued that parties are the solution to individual legislators' problems as they face election campaigns and attempt to build their careers. Responding to the near-hegemony of the Downs–Aldrich approach, in the 1990s a group of political scientists working mainly out of UCLA reimported groups into the study of parties, but as internal components of parties as "long coalitions."

With their habitual practice of slicing the study of politics into neat and manageable sectors, both groups of scholars elided the role of movements in their studies of elections and party systems.[20] For example, when Doug McAdam and I searched the index of the *Oxford Handbook of Comparative Politics* (Boix 2009), we found subject headings for elections and electoral

---

[20] The UCLA group attached "activists" to the "policy-seekers" who were the main actors in their intraparty model, but these were never connected to social movements.

systems – but none for social movements (McAdam and Tarrow 2010). Social movements were "the phantom at the opera" of public politics (Tarrow 1990).

Conversely, the 1960s wave of contention and the "new social movements" that followed led many social movement scholars to conclude that parties are cranky conservative institutions (Touraine 1971; Melucci 1980; Offe 1985) that needed to be examined separately from movements. The index to the first edition of *The Blackwell Companion to Social Movements* (Snow et al. 2004), arguably the definitive American sourcebook on the subject, included exactly two page listings for the term "elections."[21] As Daniel Gillion writes, "Historians and sociologists have explored protest and social movements, but they have largely focused on movements' origins or what sustains them; they rarely draw political connections to electoral outcomes, leaving this terrain for political scientists" (2020:9–10).

To some extent, this gap was a natural outcome of diverging methodological practices. After the appearance of *The American Voter* (Campbell et al. 1960), electoral studies were reshaped around survey methodology, which only taps into movements through the reports of surveyed individuals. More recently, a few scholars endeavored to use survey methods to study both protesting and voting behavior (Aytaç and Stokes 2019; Klandermans 2018), and a small but significant literature has adapted survey technology to the study of protesters in the act of protesting (for representative examples, see Fisher 2018 and 2000).

During the 1970s, Charles Tilly (1983) and John McCarthy and Mayer Zald (1977) began to study both protest events and social movement organizations (SMOs) with different empirical methods. While voter surveys focus on individual decision-making, protest event analysts such as Tilly collected systematic data on collective actions (Hutter 2014; Bremer et al. 2020b) and students of movement organizations such as McCarthy and Zald studied the mobilizing structures that enable such actions (Minkoff 1995; Zald and McCarthy 1987). These different methodological vectors made it difficult for students of movements and students of elections to build a unified field that brought together parties, movements, and institutions.

But in part because of the fractured state of American politics today, this separation between party and movement research is no longer tenable. These advances can partly be explained by the advent of "movement-parties." This concept first grew popular among political scientists in Europe, as the work of Herbert Kitschelt (2006) and Donatella della Porta and her collaborators (2017) attest. But it was familiar to scholars of Latin America after the rise of the

---

[21] The second edition of the *Blackwell Companion* (Snow et al. 2018) is far more ecumenical in this respect than the first, a volume that was more "social movement-centered."

Workers' Party (PT) in Brazil, and of a group of Indigenous-based parties in the Andes in the 1990s. Seeing something resembling movements within parties brought American scholars into dialogue with these comparative scholars. Starting at the turn of the new century, this led to a growing attempt to fuse the two fields into a broader field of contentious politics (Aminzade et al. 2001; McAdam et al. 2001; Goldstone et al. 2003).

2 Moves Toward Fusion

It was only in the new century that the idea of movements within parties began to influence the work of scholars of American politics, such as Daniel Gillion (2020), Doug McAdam and Karina Kloos (2014), Daniel Schlozman (2015), and Sidney Milkis and Daniel Tichenor (2019). The first moves toward fusion between movement studies and party scholarship came from movement scholars, the second from scholars of political parties, and the third from students of American political development.

Coming from Social Movements

Early pathbreakers in the social movement field were McAdam, Frances Fox Piven, and Richard Cloward. McAdam's history of the civil rights movement was impregnated with evidence of that movement's relations to the party system (1999b), while Piven and Cloward moved from an emphasis on the weight of public policy on the poor (1972) to analyzing the costs and benefits of political involvement on social movements (1977). Then McAdam – writing with Kloos – linked parties to movements in the post-1960s decades in their book *Deeply Divided* (2014). Unlike political scientists who saw polarization as a largely horizontal property, McAdam and Kloos gave polarization both a social and a political meaning, as movement activists filtered into the two major parties, assisted by such innovations as the direct primary, which had come out of the turbulence of the early 1970s.

In the 1990s, other movement scholars – such as Edwin Amenta and his collaborators – developed the concept of "political mediation," which signified the intervening institutional agents that either make it possible for movements to influence policy or stand in their way (Amenta et al. 2005; Amenta 2006). Amenta was persuaded that American parties were traditionally shy about intervening in policy because of their patronage orientation. But starting with the New Deal, the growing links between the labor movement and the Democrats and the diffusion of movements like the Townsend clubs produced a convergence between movements and institutional actors. "The Townsend

Plan," writes Amenta, "had its greatest influence when it was able to match its action appropriately to the political situation at hand" (2006:11).

Around the turn of the century, movement scholars began to examine the policy outcomes of movement activity, leading to a vast literature, best summarized in the work of Marco Giugni and his collaborators (Giugni and Yamasaki 2009; Giugni, McAdam, and Tilly 1999a and b). But measuring the outcomes of movements in terms of policy outcomes narrows the range of their possible consequences for politics (Giugni 2008:7). While Amenta's "political mediation" model focused on the regime in power and the domestic bureaucracy as "mediating" actors (Giugni 2008:8), we need to know more about the intervening role of movements and parties as interlocutors in the struggle to achieve collective goods.[22]

For example, the simplest factor that influences when parties will serve as brokers between movements and policy outputs is the strength of the party system. Strong parties have the capacity to ignore or select among movement claims, while weak parties are more likely to embrace them or risk standing aside while movements influence decision-makers. When party systems are weakened, as the American one was in the 1850s, or when they remain fully committed to an alignment structure that has become less relevant, as happened in Europe and Latin America in the 1980s and 1990s (della Porta et al. 2017; Anria 2019), political space is opened for social movements. Such interactions make clear why it is fruitful to engage the literatures on political parties and on social movements with each other.

A step toward connecting movements to the party system came in the 1960s and 1970s with the concept of "political opportunity structure" (Eisinger 1973). In the 1980s, Herbert Kitschelt used the concept as a framework for studying different forms of social movement interaction with politics (1986). Because of the greater frequency of party system change in European and Latin American history, scholars on those continents enjoyed a richer tradition of linking movements to parties and to the broader political system than Americans.

In the 1990s, Hanspeter Kriesi (1995) and Kriesi and his collaborators (1995) nested their studies of protest events within four different systems of political cleavages. In Germany, Felix Kolb studied the European antinuclear movements and the American civil rights movement in a political opportunity

---

[22] Amenta gestures toward the role of the Democratic party in the New Deal when he points out that "US programs benefiting the aged may have come as a result of the Depression or the rise to power of the Democratic Party rather than the Townsend Plan" (2005:30), but it is not clear from his account whether it was party leaders, bureaucrats, or the regime as a whole that explained the outcomes he studied.

framework (2007). Also in Germany, Dieter Rucht built a massive protest event dataset that has been the source of rich studies of movement politics ever since (Rucht and Ohlemacher 1992). More recently, both Donatella della Porta and Mario Diani founded what by now is an "Italian school" of social movement studies (2006). At the European University Institute, Kriesi and his collaborators have taken protest event analysis to a new level of methodological sophistication (Bremer et al. 2020a; Kriesi et al. 2019; 2020).

These shifts in scholarly attention had a rich counterpart in Latin America. In Brazil, Margaret Keck (1992) and Wendy Hunter (2011) studied the transformation of a workers' movement into the PT. In Central America, Paul Almeida (2008; 2010) showed how guerrilla movements emerged in the context of weak party systems. In Bolivia, Santiago Anria (2019) showed how – even after it became a fully developed party – the MAS retained many of the features of a movement. In Chile, Sofia Donoso and Marisa von Bülow and their collaborators made the relations between movements, parties, and the state central to their examination of that country's contentious politics (2017). In Latin America in general, Kenneth Roberts showed how economic liberalization provided a political opportunity for movements in countries in which the party system had been severely weakened (2015).

This work in Europe and Latin America showed that through the links between movements and parties, social change is transformed into political dynamics. Indeed, as Steffen Blings shows in his research on the German and Swedish Greens, "the saturated party systems in Europe empower social movement organizations vis-à-vis the parties they spawned, *allowing movements to hold parties programmatically to account*" (Blings 2020:220, italics added). More recently, the study of populism has questioned the traditional division of parties into left and right and shown how new alignments have left the mainstream parties ill-equipped to deal with them (Mudde and Rovira Kaltwasser 2012).

Coming from Political Parties

Parties are one of the most well-studied actors in political systems, ranging from the institutional studies of the late nineteenth and first half of the twentieth century, to more informal studies such as those of Key (1955 and 1984). Since parties are multifaceted and exist in virtually all political systems, much of the research in this field has been descriptive and typological – that is, until rational choice theory offered a way of narrowing the focus from party organizations and from "the party in the electorate" to elected elites. Following the lead of economist Anthony Downs (1957) and centering on the irreducible minimum of what parties do – namely, try to get elected – scholars such as John Aldrich posited that parties can be defined as office-seeking assemblages (1995).

David Truman, who had launched the pluralist tradition in the 1950s, observed that interest groups were leery of becoming too closely associated with a particular party (1951). Unlike the pluralists, the UCLA scholars put groups of "policy-demanders" at the center of party coalitions (Bawn et al., 2012; also see Cohen 2008). As two close observers of the UCLA school summarize:

> In making nominations, the groups that constitute parties define basic party positions, decide how much risk to take in pursuit of those positions, and choose which candidate to put forward under the party banner. Where Downs and Aldrich give primacy to office holders, the [UCLA-based] theory of parties sees successful politicians primarily as reliable agents of the groups that constitute the party" (McCarty and Schickler 2018:176–177).

For the UCLA scholars, parties were essentially "long coalitions" of groups who compose and compromise their differences through "invisible primaries" in order to win elections.[23]

The UCLA model was built on the centrality of internal policy-demanding groups and the negotiation of their demands into a party program. What it largely neglected was the role of ideology in shaping the configuration of groups in the corona of a party, regarding a party as the negotiated agreement between different groups of policy-demanders. Their approach also elided the role of parties as intermediaries between social movements and the state (McCarty and Schickler 2018).

The UCLA group's contribution to the theory of parties has been substantial. Yet although it is a deeper and more variegated model than the one that preceded it, it remained an *intra*-party model that made little of parties' relations to institutions, to the voters, and to social movements. As McCarty and Schickler put it, for the UCLA group, "Rather than being a separate, intermediary institution, the party is the sum of the bargains made by the groups that compose it" (2018:184). The model gestures toward "activists" (Bawn et al., 2012:575), but it is hard to see where social movements fit, because movements' claims frequently encompass broad ideological systems, loyalty to followers, and a dislike for transactional politics. It would take more deliberately comparative/historical approaches to tease out the various relations between parties and movements.

---

[23] To the categories of "policy seekers," Hans Noel added ideologies (2012, 2014), and Rachel Blum added "insurgent factions" (2020: ch. 1), by which she means something like internal movements.

Ideological Republicans and Group-Centered Democrats

What the Downs/Aldrich and UCLA approaches had in common was their examination of the party system within a single logic. But are the two parties really so similar? In contrast to both of these models, once we take ideology and movement linkages as independent factors and place both sets of actors in history, we will see that while they respond to each other, Republicans and Democrats have different relations over time to ideologies and interest groups.

Matt Grossmann and David Hopkins captured an important part of this difference when they distinguished between "ideological" Republicans and "group-centered" Democrats in their book, *Asymmetric Politics* (2016). Grossmann and Hopkins argued that while the Democrats are structured as a coalition of interests, the Republicans are structured by ideology. While Democratic candidates have "an incentive to base their campaigns around advocacy of specific domestic policy programs," they write, Republican candidates "stress more general rhetorical themes of small government, nationalism, and traditional morality" (Grossmann and Hopkins 2016:11). Of course, these relations to ideology and movements have not been static. As I argue below and in associated work (Tarrow 2021), each of the two parties has had a shifting relationship to both. For example, while the new Republican Party was founded on strong ideological antislavery lines, by the mid-1870s it had become essentially a party of business (Vallely 2004); and while the Democratic Party remained a party of territorial ideology for most of the period after the Civil War, the New Deal transformed it into a coalition of labor and minorities, alongside the remnants of the Solid South.

While the Democrats expanded their base by a gradual process of the accretion of new interest groups, the GOP after the 1960s was infiltrated by a sequence of social movements and movement-like organizations. When we turn later in this Element to the relationship of both parties to these ley variables, we will see mounting evidence for the "movementization" of the Republicans faced by the continued group-structuration of the Democrats.

The new century brought a number of new moves toward the fusion of political party and social movement studies, both in the United States and comparatively. First in the field was Charles Tilly, whose work since the 1970s linked parties and movements in what he called a "polity model" (Tilly 1978). Then, in the field Americans refer to as "American Political Development" (APD), a group of scholars employing historical materials could not help but notice that "critical junctures" in American history were marked by complex interactions between movements and parties. Together, these efforts provide us with the foundations for a dynamic examination of the ways in which these collective actors intersect with institutions.

Tilly and "Contentious Politics"

The first extended effort to bring together movements with other forms of political conflict came from students working with Tilly using the broad concept of "contentious politics" (McAdam et al. 2001) and by a group of scholars led by Jack Goldstone (2003). By "contentious politics" these authors meant "interactions in which actors make claims bearing on other actors' interests, leading to coordinated efforts on behalf of shared interests or programs, in which governments are involved as targets, initiators of claims, or third parties" (Tilly and Tarrow 2015:7). Contentious politics thus comprises a wide range of actors and forms of action, ranging from revolutions and civil war on one side to relatively contained forms of action like legal suits, petitions, and leafletting on the other.

Within that broad range of action, movements were defined as sustained campaigns of claim-making, using repeated performances that advertise the claim, based on the organizations, networks, traditions, and solidarities that sustain these activities (Tilly and Tarrow 2015:145). That is the definition that will inform this study: movements are a part – but only a part – of the broader field of contentious politics, which can range from anomic groups to civil society associations, nonprofits, NGOs, and even, at times, political parties. Though movements are most often associated with disruptive forms of collective action, they also engage in conventional behavior, including, increasingly, in elections (McAdam and Tarrow 2010).

For Tilly and his collaborators, movements operate through a variety of "repertoires of contention," in which some performances are forbidden, others are permitted, and still others are required. Repertoires are not only what people do but also what they *know how to do* (Tilly 2006) and what their interlocutors will recognize. Repertoires range on a spectrum from "no repertoires" to "weak repertoires" to "strong repertoires" to "rigid" ones. "Strong repertoires," writes Tilly, "imply great embedding of contention in previously existing history, culture, and social relations" (2006:41).

Movements are most visible when they engage in transgressive forms of contention, but they also put a great deal of effort into recruiting members, creating networks with other groups, and educating the public. Many of these activities overlap with those of other collectivities, ranging from unorganized mobs to interest groups to political parties. While traditional scholars tended to draw a sharp line between the performances of movements and parties, as we will see, this line is increasingly blurred and some of these performances overlap. And while movement activities are usually viewed as operating outside the range of institutions, some of their activities take place within institutions, which is where they are most likely to overlap with parties.

But it is a mistake to see movements simply as "parties in the making" or to reduce them to the status of an interest group. One of the recurring divisions between parties and movements is that while the former tend to be transactional in their relations with opponents and allies, the latter are more deeply committed to their beliefs and are likely to interpret transactions as betrayals. As Gregg Cantril wrote of the relations between the late-nineteenth-century agrarian movement and the People's Party:

> Movements create an ideology and then set concrete goals that their adherents believe can and must be achieved . . . By contrast, parties, or at least success-ful ones, create more or less stable bureaucratic structures that address the needs of individuals and of the various interest groups that comprise the electorate. (Cantrell 2020: 254–255)

But something was missing in the work of Tilly and his collaborators: the state, to which Tilly had devoted a great deal of his attention in previous works (1990, 1995). Another way of putting this is that their book *Dynamics of Contention* (2001) was so focused on the mechanisms that drive contentious politics that they elided the function of political institutions in directing move-ments either to ally with parties or to challenge them.[24]

A lacuna like this could not be ignored, and in work related to the *Dynamics* project, Goldstone and his collaborators endeavored to embed the relations between movements and parties in an institutional framework. For example, in his contribution to their book, Joseph Luders showed that local officials responded to the sit-in movement in the South to end segrega-tion in local businesses "less to the general interest in defending Jim Crow against federal incursion and more to their specific local political incentives" (2003, p. 211). But Goldstone and his collaborators did not offer any general mechanisms for how movements, parties, and the state intersect. Efforts to do so had to await the work of scholars in the field of American Political Development.

Schlozman, Rosenfeld, and the "Anchoring" of Movements

As the UCLA school was moving beyond elite-centered models of political parties, and McAdam and his collaborators were searching for generalizations about what they called "contentious politics," APD scholars were exploring the

---

[24] This was a lacuna that Tilly partially filled in a subsequent book, *Regimes and Repertoires* (2006), which he called an "orphan" of the *Dynamics* project, but that book operated at too high a level of comparison to specify how particular institutions – such as parties, legislatures, and executives – intervene between movements and institutions.

historical links between movements, parties, and the state.[25] This was, in part, a result of the changes in party/movement relations in the early twenty-first century. In this respect, I can do no better than quote the judgment of two APD scholars, Daniel Schlozman and Sam Rosenfeld:

> The nascent mobilizations of the twenty-first century – Dreamers, Occupy, Black Lives Matter, and also the Tea Party and the Alt Right – have generated energy aplenty ... As a general matter ... while movements have reason to preserve their autonomy and parties to steer clear of doctrinaire elements that threaten electoral majorities, alliance between parties and movements not only generates votes on Election Day but institutionalizes movements' cadres and priorities once the initial ardor has faded. (2019:138)

Schlozman's study of the "anchoring" of movements into parties took the study of movement/party relations into a comparative-historical study, *When Movements Anchor Parties* (2015). The two main examples he used to illustrate "anchoring" were between organized labor and the Democratic Party in the New Deal era (ch. 3) and between the Republicans and the Christian Right in the 1980s (ch. 4).

In companion efforts to his book, writing with Rosenfeld, Schlozman argued that the "anchoring" process was advanced by the "hollowing out" of political party organizations (2019), and that the interactions between a particular party and the movement sector needs to be seen over a longer historical period than we typically find in either the social movement or the political party fields. They also examined the "long" conservative movement in the United States, beginning in the 1950s with the McCarthy anti-Communist crusade, continuing through the Goldwater and Christian conservative movement and its relations to the Reagan administration, to the Tea Party and Koch network-related right-wing groups (2018).

These movement/party linkages exerted a long-term influence on party organizations and ideologies and – more broadly – on the development of the American political regime as a whole. "Repeatedly," writes Schlozman,

> movements have redefined the fundamental alignments of political parties and, in turn, the organizable alternatives in national politics. The alliances between labor and the Democrats, and the Christian Right and the Republicans have defined parties' basic priorities, and exerted long-term influence away from the median voter ... Still more important, they diverged

---

[25] From an insurgency against the largely ahistorical orientation of the mainstream of American politics in the 1970s, APD has become so widely diffused that it is difficult to find a single literature review that effectively captures its main strands. For the best such effort, see Richard Vallely, Suzanne Mettler and Robert Lieberman, eds., *The Oxford Handbook of American Political Development* (2016).

sharply from those of major social movements that *failed to find and to maintain* a stable place inside political parties. (2015: 3 [emphasis added])

I have emphasized "failed to find and to maintain" in Schlozman's summary because of what seems to me an excessive narrowing of the mission of social movements: *forging an alignment with a political party*. First, this seems to me to be to be a very "American" framing of the relation between movements and parties; for example, in America's two-party system, movements that do not forge an enduring alliance with a party tend to "fail." Second, it elides the fact that movements decide *whether or not* to aim at such an alliance. Many movements do not have political aims in the first place and, for many that do, their aim is to *rival* party elites rather than combine with them. Moreover, Schlozman's "anchoring" mechanism leaves uncertain who is the "anchor" and who is the "ship" in any such relationship.

Finally, although it is historically rooted, Schlozman's account paid little attention to the role of institutional change in shaping the relations between movements and parties. For example, the growth of the executive state since the New Deal has directed much partisan activity away from state and local party organizations to the national state (Jacobs et al. 2019). Similarly, the direct primary that was generalized by the McGovern-Fraser reforms opened the gates for movement activists to influence the nominations process at the base of the parties (Shafer 1983). This takes us to a third effort to link parties and movements to one another.

Movements, Presidents, and Parties

In their important book, *Rivalry and Reform: Presidents, Social Movements, and the Transformation of American Politics* (2019), Sidney Milkis and Daniel Tichenor take off from the relationship between Lincoln and the abolitionists – which they call "The Crucible" of movement/president relations (chapter 2) – and moves steadily toward the present, with substantial chapters on the Progressives' relation to President Theodore Roosevelt (ch. 3), the relationship between Lyndon B. Johnson and the Civil Rights movement (ch. 4), Ronald Reagan's relationship to the new Christian Right (ch. 6), and the interactions between social movements and the Obama presidency (ch. 7). Not only that: unlike the "movement output" literature, which focuses on the one-way street from movements to policy, the authors follow Tilly's (2006) call for a *relational* analysis of states and social movements, specifying that relationship through the reciprocal relations between movements and the presidency.

The overall argument of the book follows from its title. While "Lincoln and the abolitionists collaborated in a political order of highly decentralized and intensely mobilized political parties that animated a party realignment and circumscribed national administrative power"(Milkis and Tichenor 2019:283), they write, from the Progressive Era onward innovations in both the presidency and in social movements reshaped their relational dynamics. "These innovations," they argue, "have made modern presidents a more prominent and regular target of insurgents and, in turn, gave the White House fresh incentives to stay on top of potent social movements, to try to control them, and sometimes to partner with them" (pp. 6–7). "Along the way, the worlds of these often distant actors increasingly overlapped as the size and scope of presidential power and particular movements grew" (pp. 6–7).

Milkis and Tichenor did their historical homework well, with forty-eight pages of densely sourced endnotes covering both the secondary literature and original archival work. But, more important, their narratives were shaped by a theoretically honed typology linking the type of movement challenges to different forms of institutional responses (p. 19). The movement/presidential "rivalries and reforms" they found in their histories were motivated by the variations and combinations that emerged from their typology. Table 1 adapts their typology to the broader issue of the relations between movements and institutions.

Each one of the "cells" of Milkis and Tichenor's typology can be illustrated by different examples of movement/presidential relations in American political development. An example of what they call a *marginal movement*, one to which there was only a cursory presidential response, is the Occupy Movement of

Table 1 Movement Challenges and Institutional Responses: Linking Conventional and Disruptive Movement Capacities

	Significant tactical challenge	*Insignificant tactical challenge*
Insignificant Conventional Political Leverage	Militant Movements	Marginal Movements
significant Conventional Political Leverage	Formative Movements	Institutionalized Movements

Source: Adapted from Sidney M. Milkis and Daniel J. Tichenor, *Rivalry and Reform: Presidents, Social Movements and the Transformation of American Politics*, U.of Chicago Press, 2019, p. 19.

2011–2012; the case of a *militant movement* that triggered a forceful presidential response is the Animal Rights Militia of the 2000s; that of an *institutionalized movement* that led to a co-optive presidential response is the New Christian Right of the 1980s; and that of a *formative movement* that produced a forceful presidential response is the LGBTQ rights movement of the last few decades. The most successful "formative" movement in American history was, of course, the civil rights movement, which combined institutional, quasi-institutional, and contentious forms of action during its long history.

The advantage of Milkis and Tichenor's theoretical architecture is that it allowed them to examine different configurations of the interactions between presidents and activists. The book's most important contribution is to show how the growing power of the executive in the twentieth century both built upon and advanced changes in movements that made claims on presidential power. For example, Lyndon B. Johnson's quasi-alliance with the moderate, southern-born sector of the Civil Rights movement was triggered by that movement's demonstrated power to disrupt but also helped to divide it, as leaders such as Martin Luther King, Jr. were outflanked from their left by a new generation of (mainly northern) young black leaders.

But factional divisions, Milkis and Tichenor argue, are not always negative for a movement's relations to the party system. For example, in their account of the abolitionists' uneasy relationship with Lincoln, the authors show that the antislavery cause was in fact advanced by its divisions: the "outsider" abolitionists actually complemented the efforts of "insider" Radical Republicans (2019:59; also see Tarrow 2021: ch. 1). But their book also shows how movement/presidential alliances can prove ephemeral. After the passage of the Reconstruction amendments, the Republican coalition was shattered by its internal differences and by the agreement of 1876, which threw the South back into the pocket of former secessionists.

The story of the death of the antislavery movement after the end of the Civil War illustrates one of the book's major themes – that important movements can only be understood by taking a long historical view. Their longue-durée framework helped Milkis and Tichenor both to encompass recurrent patterns of presidential/movement interaction and to focus on the layering of emergent forms of interaction upon existing ones (2019:33). For example, they show how, during the New Deal, movement/presidential relations laid the foundation for strengthening of the civil rights movement that came to fruition only in the 1950s and 1960s (Schickler 2016).[26] The weakening of the party system over

---

[26] *Rivalry and Reform* (2019) also laid the groundwork for successive work by Milkis and collaborators on the decline of the "vital center' of the American party system" (Jacobs and Milkis 2022).

time was one of the main sources of the increased interaction between move-ments and institutions. As the executive grew in power and new forms of participation grew up alongside parties, the parties themselves were increas-ingly "hollowed out" (Schlozman and Rosenfeld 2019:138), leaving space for the partial "movementization' of the party system (Tarrow 2018) and for outsider groups – like the Koch Network – (Skocpol and Hertel-Fernandez 2016a and b) to infiltrate and to some extent capture the Republican party (Perlstein 2009; 2020).

Like all four-cell typologies, the theoretical framework of Milkis and Tichenor's book was built on two foundational variables: the degree of tactical movement challenge and the degree of conventional leverage employed by a movement (2019:19). What the typology leaves out, however, are variables that mediate between movement claims and presidential response – such as the party system.[27] The author of the classic *The President and the Parties* (Milkis 1993) and the winner of the Jack Walker Award for an article of unusual significance to the field of political parties and organizations (Tichenor 2003) obviously know a lot about president/party relations. But while there are parties aplenty in the empirical chapters of *Rivalry and Reform*, their absence from the authors' theoretical framework leaves the issue of party mediation between presidencies and movements somewhat under-theorized.

For example, Lincoln's relations with the abolitionist movement were medi-ated by the radical faction in the Republican Party. FDR's uneasy relations with the civil rights movement were mediated by a Democratic party that was hamstrung by the weight of the solid South within the party in Congress, as Ira Katznelson's *Fear Itself* (2013) demonstrates. Lyndon Johnson's embrace of that movement was mediated by his effort to replace the Democrats' disappear-ing white southern base with African-American voters. And the growing influ-ence of Tea Party–backed representatives in Congress weakened the influence of the moderate branch of the Republican Party and helps to explain the nomination of an ideological intruder in the 2016 election.

That said, the modern presidency, with its growing relationship to movement organizations, has been a critical factor both in weakening the parties and in exacerbating partisanship. This double trend first emerged in Johnson's rela-tionship with the movements of the 1960s. It was advanced by the changes in the party nominations system after the McGovern reforms (Shafer 1983; Mcadam and Kloos 2014). It took root in the Republican Party with the entry of the New Right and the Christian conservatives into that party. And it reached its

---

[27] For a convincing effort to insert political parties between movemetns and presidencies, see Sidney Milkis and Daniel Tichenor, "When revolutions go backward: Democratic precarity in American political development," unpublished paper, 2021.

culmination in the insertion of the Tea Party into the GOP, with the financial power of the Koch network behind it (Gervais and Morris 2018). "These changes," Milkis and Tichenor conclude, "were a response to, and further advanced, the decline of regular party organizations, giving rise to an unfiltered partisanship that sharpened political conflict and rattled national resolve" (2019:304).

These efforts were important steps in constructing an encompassing framework for the study of movement/party relations. But none of them offers a dynamic, interactive approach that we can employ to map the variety of movement/party relations and their changes over time. Nor do they allow us to understand the patterns of these relations in the twenty-first century. That will be the goal of the remainder of this Element.

3 Movement/Party Relations in Critical Junctures[28]

Movements – to adopt Tilly's language – both shape and are shaped by changes in regimes – and not always in cooperative ways. But these relations became more intimate and more interactive during the "critical junctures" of American history: From Lincoln's intermittent relationships with activists such as Frederick Douglass to Wilson's strained relations with the suffragists and FDR's relations with the Congress of Industrial Organizations (CIO), presidential/movement interactions evolved toward Lyndon Baines Johnson's partly cooperative and partly competitive interactions with leaders such as Martin Luther King, Jr. From there they evolved to Reagan's carefully staged, but cautious alliance with the New Christian Right, to Obama's efforts to create his own movement infrastructure around Organizing for Action (Milkis and York 2017), and then to Trump's insertion of the logic of his nationalist/exclusionary movement into the heart of the presidency.

In the remainder of this Element, drawing on a larger comparative-historical study of the intersection of movements and parties during major "critical junctures" in American history (Tarrow 2021), I will specify five major mechanisms that connect parties to movements: two of them short range, two others in the intermediate range, and the fifth over the long run. But before turning to these mechanisms, a brief outline of the concept of "critical junctures" will be useful to lay the groundwork for the analysis to follow. I will argue that critical junctures are "the crucibles" within which these actors interact and from which new phases of party/movement relations ensue.

---

[28] Much of this section draws on my work with Doug McAdam (McAdam and Tarrow 2010) and on my book, *Movements and Parties in American Political Development* (2021) from which this Element is drawn.

Critical Junctures

The concept of critical junctures comes from a tradition in comparative politics, first reflected in the work of Seymour Martin Lipset and Stein Rokkan (1967) and then in a major study of Latin America by David and Ruth Collier (1991). The concept has most recently been revitalized by David Collier and Gerardo Munck in a 2017 collective work and in a collective book in progress.[29]

The concept is not entirely foreign to American politics but has often been narrowed to that of critical *elections*. For example, Walter Dean Burnham (1970) defined critical junctures as periods marked by major electoral realignments – among them the realigning election of 1860, the beginning of a new party system in 1896, and the start of the New Deal coalition in 1932. But a moment's reflection should tell us that elections are not always the centerpieces of periods of dramatic change. Wars, revolutions, and economic crises also give rise to increased interactions between parties and movements. Critical junctures are broader than electoral shifts, arise from a combination of structural change and political processes, and have long legacies that are often unexpected when the episode begins.

In a recent effort inspired by the Colliers' work, Munck defined critical junctures as

> a rapid discontinuous change at the macro-level of organization of society; and, as such, is a qualitative novelty that marks a before and after and that provides a basis for identifying a point of entry into the stream of history. (Munck, in preparation, p. 4)

Phases of Critical Junctures

The first important way to examine such junctures is to begin with the "antecedent conditions" that lay the groundwork for them. For example, V.O. Key saw the wellspring of the New Deal coalition already in the 1928 election (Key 1955). These can be either changes in embedded cleavages or "eventful" events that trigger a cascade of other changes, leading to the shock or crisis at the peak of the juncture. For example, the critical election of 1860 can only be understood in the light of the breakdown of the "balance rule" in Congress and the resulting rise of the Republican Party from a coalition of Democratic, Whig, and Free Soil activists (Tarrow 2021:ch. 1).

---

[29] Their wide-ranging book in progress, *Critical Junctures and Historical Legacies: Insights and Tools for Comparative Social Science* (in press), aims at both theoretical and empirical progress in employing the concept of critical junctures. I am grateful to Collier and Munck for allowing me to consult and quote from their work.

The second phase is the peak of the juncture. Kenneth Roberts describes such periods as "periods of crisis or strain that existing policies and institutions are ill-suited to resolve" (2015: 65). The Civil War was certainly such a shock, but so was the onset of the Great Depression and the period beginning with the attacks on the World Trade Center and the Pentagon in 2001.

"Shocks" are often "syncretic," as these episodes suggest, but they can also be "incremental," in which more than one crisis is layered upon and intersects with existing ones. It may well turn out that the coronavirus pandemic of 2020 will be seen in the future as a new layer of crisis upon the collapse of the traditional Republican Party that was marked by Donald Trump's ascendance and the racial justice crisis that began with the murder of Trayvon Martin in 2013.

Third is the legacy of the critical juncture. Collier and Collier noted that "To the extent that the critical juncture is a polarizing event that produces intense political reactions and counterreactions, the crystallization of the legacy does not necessarily occur immediately, but rather may consist of a sequence of intervening steps that respond to these reactions and counterreactions" (Collier and Collier 1991:37). That legacy can be direct – like the Reconstruction period that followed the Civil War – but it often produces "reactive sequences" "marked by backlash processes that can *transform* and perhaps *reverse* early events" (Mahoney 2000:367), like the white "redemption" of the South after Reconstruction.

Critical junctures are sometimes coterminous with new social movements and with new "anchorings" between movements and parties. The New Deal was a prime example of both, in which a new branch of the labor movement – the CIO – broke away from the traditional American Federation of Labor and forged an integral tie with the Democratic Party. But critical junctures also produce linkages between *existing* movements and parties, as was the case for the connection between the Civil Rights movement and the Democrats in the 1960s.

Civil rights was a "long" movement that existed well before the Democrats transformed into a moderately liberal party, just as the conservative "New Right," which arose in the 1950s and 1960s, was only "anchored" to the Republican Party during the subsequent decades (Schlozman and Rosenfeld 2019). The intersection between "long movements" and shorter critical junctures makes the study of political development both interesting and complex.[30]

During critical junctures, the interactions between movements and parties intensify, institutional and noninstitutional conflicts intersect, people who have

---

[30] I am grateful to Dan Tichenor for pointing this out to me in a thoughtful reading of a draft of this paper.

entered public life through movements gravitate into parties, and parties shift their ground to embrace new issues and attract new supporters. In such periods, parties and movements relate to each other in more intimate ways than in less momentous times, through both rivalry and cooperation (Milkis and Tichenor 2019). The result is to infuse institutional politics with the passions – and the divisions – of movement politics, leaving a legacy that crystallizes in the party system and often leaves a permanent mark on the institutions of government.

The most *proactive* way in which movements influence parties is through elections. Movements can introduce new forms of collective action that influence election campaigns; they can join electoral coalitions; and, in extreme cases, they turn into parties themselves (McAdam and Tarrow 2010). The formation of the "New Deal" coalition after FDR's election in 1932 was such a moment, although it was presaged by the election of 1928 (Key 1955) and followed by the 1936 election in which African Americans began to defect from their traditional loyalty to the "party of Lincoln" (Schickler 2016) into a lasting "anchoring" to the Democratic Party.

A second and *reactive* way in which movement actions influence elections and parties is the formation of a "countermovement," which can take violent, organizational, or even institutional forms. The most violent was the creation of the Ku Klux Klan to combat the gains that African Americans were making during reconstruction; possibly the most substantial organizational reaction was the creation of the National Association for the Advancement of Colored People (NAACP) in response to the wave of lynchings in the South in the early twentieth century (Francis 2014); and arguably the most substantial institutional change on movement/party relations was the generalization of the direct primary in the 1970s.

In the intermediate range, critical junctures *shape the strategies and structures of future movements.* A successful electoral intervention draws movements toward the electoral arena, and these changes can bring about a longer-term shift in movements' electoral involvement. The widespread creation of nonprofit public interest groups was a direct result of the movements of the 1960s, many of whose veterans had entered this new generation of activism during the 1970s (McAdam 1999a).

Also in the intermediate range, the interactions among movements, parties, and countermovements can *reshape political institutions.* These are often electoral institutions, but they can also be changes in the mechanisms of social control and repression, or broader changes, like the beginning of the welfare state that brought African Americans into the polity from the 1930s to the 1960s.

Finally, through this complex of interactions, in the long term, *regimes are shaped and reshaped*, often threatened, and sometimes expanded in critical junctures. Many historians – following the aphorism of Martin Luther King, Jr. that "the arc of the moral universe is long but it bends toward justice" – implicitly believe that American history is the history of democratization. Some of the critical junctures in this history – like Reconstruction and women's suffrage – did indeed "bend toward justice," but others did not, and still others produced a combination of democratizing and dedemocratizing trends.

In the remainder of this paper, I will draw on my own research and on that of others who have examined movement/party relations in American political development to illustrate how these mechanisms have worked during critical junctures in the past and suggest how they may affect democratization and dedemocratization in the future.

4 Two Short-Term Linkage Mechanisms

Most research in the social movement tradition is limited to the short-term policy results of movement mobilization (Giugni 2009). Other work examines the biographical impact of movement activity on the individuals who engage in it (McAdam 1999a). But movements seldom have so direct an influence on politics; their impact is more often mediated by institutions, parties, and the conflict structure in which they are embedded (Amenta 2005; 2006). When we specify this conflict structure, two dimensions appear to be most important: *the impact of movements on elections* and *the interaction between movements and their antagonists* – sometimes the state, but often other movements.

The Electoral Connection

Movements make three kinds of claims on authorities, all three of which become most visible when they engage in elections: *identity claims, standing claims, and program claims*. Identity claims declare that a particular actor exists, standing claims say that that actor deserves the rights and the recognition of recognized categories, while program claims call for authorities to respond to their needs in certain ways (Tilly and Tarrow 2015:110–111). We see few "pure" cases of any single type of claim, but drawing on various critical junctures in American history, we find different combinations of demands on parties and political authorities:

- The abolitionist movement and the radical faction of the Republican Party made identity and standing claims on behalf of African Americans but did not agree on a program for what would happen "after" the Civil War. That lack of clarity explains a lot of the failures of Reconstruction, as well as the inability to come to a consensus about the desirability of black enfranchisement;

- The agrarian leagues of the 1880s and 1890s sought recognition and standing for farmers as independent producers but could not come together behind a consensual program of reform or bridge the sectional and racial differences in the farm population. Their confluence within the Populist party led to an ill-starred effort to win power through an alliance with the Democrats in the 1896 election on a divisive platform of free coinage of silver;
- The woman's franchise movement had an agreed-upon programmatic goal based on the desire for women's standing as equal citizens, but included a good bit of uncertainty about women's identity;
- The civil rights movement came closest to developing a clear set of identity, standing, and program claims. But as the movement shifted from South to North and urban violence pushed its nonviolent repertoire off the pages of the media, a new generation of activists put forward more radical programmatic claims and insisted on a more distinct set of identity claims;
- The "New Right" and the Christian conservatives had distinct identity and program claims, but they were unified in seeking greater standing for those they claimed to represent through the Republican party;
- Finally, the Tea Party movement had two distinct programmatic foci – libertarian and social conservative – and a desire for greater standing in a society they saw leaving them behind (Parker and Barreto 2013).

Political regimes both limit claims and channel them toward particular forms of claim-making. While authoritarian regimes restrict even routine forms of contention – thus driving claims-makers toward more extreme measures – liberal democracies both tolerate and invite contention, thus driving claims-makers toward more institutional routines.

Political regimes limit and channel movement claims in three main ways. First, a regime's political opportunity structure affects which claims resonate and can be transformed into programs. Second, every regime divides its claims-making repertoire into prescribed, tolerated, and forbidden performances. Third, the available repertoire limits the kinds of claims people can make in any particular regime.[31]

Parties are the intermediary institutions that mediate between a regime's opportunity structure and the claims that movements put forward and the means they have available to do so.

Three types of variation in parties and party systems are the elements that either constrain or encourage movements to merge with the party system: opportunities offered to movements through electoral contests, variations in

---

[31] This argument is condensed from Tilly and Tarrow 2015:111–112.

the competitiveness of the party system, and party strength or weakness. All three of these converge in electoral contests.

Openness and Closure of Electoral Opportunities. Parties both open and close opportunities for movements at election time (McAdam and Tarrow 2010). They manage campaigns that offer movements legitimate opportunities to mobilize supporters and attract others, give them a chance to insert their issues into the electoral agenda, and direct them away from disruptive and toward conventional activities. Elections also offer opportunities for the creation of "movement-parties," which attempt to transform the ideological fervor of movement mililtants into electoral mobilization (Anria 2019).

This combination of "invitation plus domestication" appeared in each of the critical junctures above. A first example was the "balance rule" between the Democrats and the Whigs in Congress between 1820 and the early 1850s that moderated territorial and racial strife, which encouraged a split between "absolute" and "political" abolitionists and drove the latter into the new Republican Party. When the balance rule was broken in 1854, it shattered the unity of both Democrats and Whigs and led to a critical election that opened the door to the influence of the previously shunned antislavery movement.

Radical Republicans supported Lincoln in the Civil War, passed the Reconstruction Amendments opening the franchise to ex-slaves, and helped to organize them electorally through the Union Leagues. But supporting this new constituency proved both difficult and expensive, and when northern voters objected to extending the franchise to African Americans outside the South, the Republicans abandoned their new constituency to its fate. As W. E. B. Du Bois diagnosed it, black enfranchisement failed in the South, not due to African American failures, but due to the shift in strategy of the Republicans who had liberated the slaves (Du Bois 1935).

Taking Advantage of Electoral Competition. The competition for votes provide movement activists with leverage in the political system. For example, the suffragists of the late nineteenth and early twentieth centuries despised party politics but were not adverse to taking advantage of opportunities opened by elections – as they did when the western states extended the vote to women before the passage of the XIXth Amendment. It was the greater competitiveness of western party systems that allowed the movement to gain the vote in that region sooner than in either the machine-dominated North or the one-party South (Teele 2018a and b).

But after the Amendment passed in 2020, women voters turned out to be just as split on other issues as their male counterparts, and continued to divide between those – like Alice Paul and the National Women's Party – who wanted nothing less than equal rights for women – and reformers who sought incremental reforms in the workplace and in the home. It was only in the 1930s that women reformers found a home in the Democratic Party.

Civil Rights activists were also deeply affected by electoral competition. Long stymied by disenfranchisement in the South and by their stubborn loyalty to "the party of Lincoln," they began to turn to the Democrats in response to the promise of the New Deal's social programs. President Roosevelt was worried about the loss of southern support in Congress if he showed too much interest in black rights, but many New Dealers and militant unionists forged an alliance with the movement that ripened during the last part of the 1930s, went on hold during World War Two, and was revived during the Cold War (Schickler 2016; Dudziak 2000). The impending shift of the white South to the Republicans after the passage of the Civil Rights and Voting Rights Acts in the mid-1960s laid the foundation for a permanent alliance between the Democrats and the Civil Rights movement. So deep was the alliance between the movement and the party that some analysts argued that the Democrats had "captured' the votes of African Americans (Frymer 1999).

Party Strength and Weakness. Party weakness or strength is a third factor that implicates the entry of social movements into the party system. Weakened parties offer inviting openings for movement activists, while strong parties can remain indifferent to movements' claims. In the 1890s, after almost unbroken Republican rule since the Civil War, the Democrats' electoral base was largely restricted to the South and to the immigrant vote in the North. Seeking to expand it into the Republican heartland, the party nominated William Jennings Bryan for the Presidency in 1896, who tried to bolster his chances by an alliance with the Populists. Although Bryan continued to run for president into the new century, the Populists – and the agrarian leagues within them – crashed and burned soon after.

The appeal of adding women as a new voting bloc attracted the Republicans in the early 1920s. Weakened by eight years of Democratic rule under Woodrow Wilson, party leaders worried about the unknown effects of the women's vote. As a result, they supported reforms pushed by the women's lobby. But as women turned out to be both divided and low-turnout voters, by the mid-1920s the party felt strong enough to ignore women's issues. By the mid-1930s, the woman's movement had largely given up on the GOP and shifted sharply to support for the Democrats.

During a second period of weakness, culminating in Johnson's crushing defeat of Goldwater in 1964, the Republicans opened up to the entry of a succession of insurgent groups, beginning with the Young Republicans after the disastrous Goldwater campaign, the Christian conservatives in the 1970s, and the Reaganites in 1980 (Perlstein 2009; 2020). Once inside that party, these insurgents turned it into a more ideological instrument, making it fair game for the Tea Party insurgency, one that was based on a combination of racial resentment, economic libertarianism, and evangelical ardor – just the combination for an ideological opportunist such as Donald Trump to manipulate and dominate. But Trump's election led to a massive resistance (Meyer and Tarrow 2018; Skocpol and Tervo 2020), which takes us to our second short-term mechanism linking parties and movements: the interaction between movements and countermovements.

Movement–Countermovement Interaction

Movements often create their own opposition, which sometimes takes countermovement form. David Meyer and Suzanne Staggenborg listed three conditions that promote the rise of countermovements (1996): First, that the movement it opposes shows signs of success; second, that the interests of some populations are threatened by movement goals; and, third, that political allies are available to aid countermovement mobilization. All three of these factors combined in the countermovement of the Ku Klux Klan against black liberation during Reconstruction.

If only because the South had been devastated by the Civil War, but also because the Republican Party enjoyed a near-monopoly of power in a much-strengthened federal government, Reconstruction threatened white power holders with the loss of their racial supremacy. But there was also a vigorous "Black Reconstruction" (Du Bois 1935; Foner 2014) that threatened even poor Whites, as the ex-slaves used their churches and military experiences to organize electorally. The success of the war and the threat to the white power structure represented by an active black electorate were two sides of the incentive for the formation of a white countermovement.

That movement took mainly violent form during Reconstruction, but after the electoral deal of 1876 that led to the withdrawal of federal forces from the South, white rule was reinstituted by increasingly white state legislatures that passed a plethora of legal and semilegal regulations designed to ensure segregation and keep African Americans from the voting booth. Though fulminating about the denial to Blacks of the Reconstruction Amendments, Republicans discovered that they could assure their electoral future through a Northern/ Western coalition of white voters in the name of ascendant capitalism.

The women's suffrage movement, which arose out of antislavery in the 1840s, triggered the organization of a countermovement in the form of the National Association Opposed to Woman Suffrage (NAOWS). In the South, these women were worried that votes for women would disrupt a social order based on white supremacy, while in the North they were mainly the daughters or wives of wealthy businessmen who were convinced that giving women the vote would end such widespread practices as child labor.

That the NAOWS was a true countermovement was indicated by the fact that it was strongest where the suffrage cause was flourishing – for example, in Massachusetts and New York City. Women who opposed votes for women emphasized the dirtiness of politics and the wish to keep women in the home, where their purity would be unsullied by contact with machine politicians.

In the 1950s and 1960s, southern segregationists responded to antisegregation court decisions and to efforts to implement African American voting rights both with new institutions, like the white Citizens' Councils, and with a resurgence of Klan violence. In the summer of 1964, when the bodies of three Student Non-Violent Coordinating Committee (SNCC) poll workers were discovered in an earthen dam in rural Mississippi, outrage over the atrocity helped to bolster northern support for the Civil Rights Act, which was passed by Congress in the same year.

But although the Klan was responsible for many murders and for the burning of black churches, more consequential politically were the white Citizen Councils that first grew up in the Deep South and then diffused throughout the region. Although the councils insisted on their legal vocation, they advanced polarization by putting pressure on moderate and integrationist groups and by enforcing economic pressure against Whites considered traitorous to southern values.

Both Council and Klan activism were instrumental in the creation of white educational academies. When, in the late 1960s, the Supreme Court decided the case of *Alexander* v. *Holmes County*, striking down Mississippi's "school choice" statute, the response was to spur white families, churches, and other institutions to create private academies in a large number of the state's counties (Andrews 2002:921–922). These academies were linked to the prior formation of the Citizens' Councils and to previous Klan activity. Kenneth Andrews also found that counties with higher levels of civil rights mobilization in the 1960s had higher academy enrollments (2002:921–922).

Perhaps the most successful countermovement in modern American history was the campaign of Phyllis Schlafly and the "STOP-ERA" movement she founded against the equal rights amendment that was the most organic reform effort of the women's movement of the 1960s and 1970s. Combining the tried-and-true methods learned in her anti-Communist past with the support of religious groups, Schlaffly turned back a near-successful state ratification process that put equal rights for women on the back burner for years after. When an anti-ERA plank was added to the platform of the Republican Party in the 1980 election, Schaffley's movement blended into the Republican party politics out of which she had come.

The most recent example of movement/countermovement interaction came before and after the election of Donald Trump to the presidency. In that period, we find evidence of all three of Meyer and Staggenborg's conditions for the formation of a countermovement.

First, Trump's electoral success was a triumph for the movement he had stimulated, followed by Republican successes in a number of by-elections that followed. Perhaps more important, Trump's populist base held firm during the first three years of his mandate, not so much because of what he had done for them, but because of the racial resentment that he was able to stoke, and because the Democrats were successfully painted as a party dominated by the interests of feminists, Hispanics, African Americans, and coastal elites.

Second, during his years in office, Trump threatened the interests and values of vast sectors of the American population, from African Americans to Latinos, women, businesses dependent on foreign trade agreements, and the LGBT community. For each major policy initiative – from his early refugee ban to his attacks on Obamacare, tax reform, and his judicial appointments – Trump's programs and rhetoric were a powerful threat to many Americans.

Third, Trump's policy excesses and his outsized personality offered a focal point for various sectors of what came to be called "The Resistance," which helped in the formation of alliances. Even his racial outbursts helped to advance black–brown and black/white alliances. "Intersectional" alliances were already visible in the various marches that Dana Fisher investigated in a series of onsite protester surveys in 2017, long before the George Floyd protests. As she wrote soon after:

> the percentaqe of repeat Resisters who have participated in the events that make up the resistance in the streets has been very high at every event. In fact, three-quarters of all participants at the March for Racial Justice, the 2018 Women's March, the March for Our Lives, and Families Belong Together event also reported attending the Women's March. (Fisher 2019:47)

The Trump presidency ignited a countermovement of heavily female, mainly middle-class Americans across the country, as Theda Skocpol and her collaborators wrote in *Upending American Democracy* (Skocpol and Tervo 2020). For example, many of the people who participated in the woman's march in 2017 went on to form grassroots anti-Trump groups. The result was the "blue wave' of Democratic victories in the 2018 midterm elections and a surge in support for the Biden campaign in the summer and fall of 2020. Both the reaction to Trumpism and the formation of the shift of the "new" women's movement were at the root of the significant shift of white female voters to the Democrats in the 2020 election.

5 Two Intermediate-Level Mechanisms

In the late 1990s a group of European and American scholars noted what they saw as the generalization – indeed, the "normalization" – of contentious forms of politics in western democracies. They called this trend the emergence of a "movement society" (Meyer and Tarrow 1998). By this term they meant not only that protest and collective action were becoming more common. That was certainly true, but they also hypothesized that these performances were becoming more familiar, more expected, and even legitimated by elites, like the strike had when collective bargaining was institutionalized.

In other words, public forms of contentious politics that are either peaceful or transgressive were becoming more familiar, standardized, and "modular" – that is, adaptable to a wide variety of sites and sectors (Tilly and Tarrow 2015:16–17). This is not the same as saying that they had become "institutionalized," but, hovering on the border between transgressive and routine repertoires, they were ripe for adaptation into the party system.

But the thesis of a "movement society" may have been too simple, for while protest – assisted by the advent of the Internet and social media – has mainly diffused in conventional forms, it has also taken disruptive and violent forms. Even more interesting, some movements became more multivalent, employing both conventional and transgressive forms, especially if we interpret that term to include the "insurgent" actions of actors whose goal is to disrupt the existing party system from within.

Consider the Tea Party (Parker and Barreto 2013; Gervais and Morris 2018). Rather than a single social movement organization, it was a loosely coupled network that consisted of grassroots cell-like chapters, deep-pocketed national conservative organizations, and media support that was so intimately interlarded with movement actions that they consisted in a virtual part of the movement's apparatus (Skocpol and Williamson 2011). What this means is that the "movement society" cannot be seen as a distinct subsystem of noninstitutional participation, but rather of hybrid forms that mobilize on the borders – and sometime within – political parties (Blum 2020). Two intermediate-range mechanisms demonstrate these linkages.

Institutional Effects of Movement Mobilization

When we turn to the impact of party/movement interactions on institutions, it is helpful to distinguish between those episodes in which movements *aim* at institutional change and those that *achieve* it as a by-product of other claims. A clear-cut episode of a movement seeking institutional change was the women's suffrage movement. This was a two-stage struggle for institutional change resulting from a "winning strategy" of, first, a state-to-state campaign, and then the national campaign for the XIXth Amendment, but it was focused on a single institutional reform.

Movements that have an indirect influence on institutions are more difficult to study because the effects of their efforts are often years or even decades in the making. To complicate the issue further, many of the institutional changes that result from such movements' activity are not the direct result of their efforts, but of the interaction between movement claims, the decisions of other actors, and their political mediation. As Tilly wryly remarked in *Regimes and Repertoires*, "Contentious politics does not ... operate like a hydraulic pump: increase the pressure or reduce the resistance and more water flows" (2006:110).

Even direct movement/institutional causal chains are not simple. For example, it took more than seventy years for the women's movement to take its final shape, expand geographically, and achieve the vote for women. That movement was also dependent on other movements – such as the Temperance movement and the Progressives – and on events outside its control – such as World War One. It depended less on its own devices than on the decisions of parties and political leaders who saw that they could no longer resist a change that had come to seem inevitable. Especially after women supported the war effort, party leaders began to line up to compete for their votes. Even President Wilson, who thought women were not suited for the suffrage, changed his mind when he saw women's suffrage creeping across the country from the West.

For decades, women had been slowly gaining the vote in the West, due mainly to political competition and to the weakness of party organizations in that region, only reaching the key northeastern states when northern Democrats came on board. The key national vote came in 1918 in the House, when the "Susan B. Anthony Amendment" received the necessary two-thirds support over the objections of southern Democrats and the opposition of a well-financed antisuffrage movement. "Political mediation" was complicated, contradictory, and slow moving, depending largely on when and where elements in the party system saw that support for the amendment held greater promise than risks.

The momentous institutional change in the growth of federal power brought on by the Civil War was also the result of party/movement interaction. That war was fought over slavery and secession. But one of the major changes it brought about was to increase the power of the national state and link it firmly to the financial sector that had financed the Union's war effort (Bensel 1990). And of course the war led to the passage of the three most significant constitutional amendments in the history of the country, which eventually forced federal institutions to line up on the side of racial equality.

Many important institutional changes occur almost as side effects of movement/party interactions over other issues. The most recent of these was the adoption of the direct presidential primary in the Democratic Party in the early 1970s and the diffusion of the practice to the Republicans soon after. That reform ultimately fed into to what I have called the "movementization" of the party system and contributed deeply to the polarization of the country's politics (Mcadam and Kloos 2014; Tarrow 2018). This was a reform that began over the seating of an African American Mississippi delegation at the 1964 convention but ended by transforming the institutional framework of candidate selection for the next half-century.

Like much else in contemporary American politics, the process began in the 1960s. As McAdam and Kloos argued in *Deeply Divided*,

> as the 1970s dawned, both parties were shifting to accommodate the mobilized movement wings at their respective margins. The Democrats were contending with the increasingly radical movements of the New Left, while the GOP moved right to court racial conservatives and other disaffected elements of the former New Deal coalition (2014:25–26).

The result of what Byron Shafer has called "the greatest systematically planned ... shift in the institutions of delegate selection in all of American history" (1983:4) gave grassroots activists the power to contest the candidate choices of party regulars. "In short," conclude McAdam and Kloos, "while reformers had sought to democratize the nominating process, the resulting system has proven to be the perfect vehicle for empowering the movement wings of the two parties" (2014:28). The episode of the reform of party nominations in the 1970s takes us to my fourth claim: that the relationship between movements and parties has grown more intimate during different stages of American political development. Although the origins of this trend can be traced to the pre-Civil War period (Tarrow 2021: ch. 1), it became inexorable with the strengthening of the national state and the hollowing-out of party organizations after World War Two.

Hollowing Parties and Strengthening Executives

For decades, American political scientists assumed that democracies around the world would roughly follow America's developmental path from parties of notables to mass parties to one or another variant of "cartel parties" (Katz and Mair 1993). Until recently, they paid little attention to the question of whether American political development might follow the paths seen in other parts of the world.[32] The only important exception were proponents of the view that American parties would do better to form "a more responsible two-party system" like the British parliamentary system that would permit a logically consistent left-versus-right dialectic of political conflict (Rosenfeld 2018).

The weakening of the American party system and the growth of more vigorous nonparty forms of participation in recent decades has raised the question of whether foreign models may be more relevant to the structure of American politics today than they were in the past. While scholars like Gabriel Almond and Sidney Verba made a sharp theoretical distinction between the process of "interest articulation" – the main function of social movements and interest groups – and "interest aggregation" – the proper function of political parties – they worried that these two functions were interlarded in the non-American cases they studied (1964). But as recent developments suggest, changes have taken place in the American party system that resemble movement/party relations in other parts of the world.

Consider the Latin American experience. Its recent history teaches that when party systems are weakened, or when they remain structured by a particular alignment structure that has become less relevant, political space is often filled by new or revitalized social movements (Roberts 2015). This is what happened in a number of Latin American party systems when their governments adopted neoliberal economic models – the so-called "Washington consensus" – in the 1990s (Roberts 2015). Some of these movements – like the Brazilian PT (Keck 1992) – transformed into full-fledged parties with oligarchical structures as they matured; others remained movement-parties, like the MAS in Bolivia (Anria 2019); in still others, as in Chile, social movements that had been deeply involved in democratic transitions relapsed into relative impotence as the party system institutionalized (Luna and Altman 2011).

American parties have not reached the degree of decay that Latin American parties did around the turn of the century, in part because neoliberalism was less of a "turn" in the United States than a long-term trend, and in part because it is harder to mount new parties in a bipolar system than in a multipolar one. But as the American parties have been "hollowed out," social movements and other nonparty vehicles began to gain purchase, both within and on the borders of the two mainstream parties. The weakening of party organizations and the strengthening

---

[32] The apogee of this Americanocentric view came in the early 1960s in the work of Gabriel Almond and Sidney Verba: *The Civic Culture* (1964).

of party-linked movements goes back to the 1960s. This was due to the entry of the New Right into the Republican party in the 1960s (Perlstein 2009), and of the Christian Right in the 1970s and 1980s (Perlstein 2020). But these were not the only "outsider" groups that have become interlopers in party politics; Barack Obama's Organizing for America was (an admittedly failed) top-down movement in the Democratic world, while both the Tea Party and the Koch Network have had a profound influence on the Republican one (Skocpol and Hertel-Ferandez 2016a and b; Blum 2020).

Critics and some analysts have dismissed such organizations as no more than "astroturf" movements to indicate the falsity of their claim to represent grass-roots society. In his important work *Grassroots for Hire* (2014), Edward Walker shows how an entire new industry has grown up to mobilize citizens on behalf of powerful firms and business associations attempting to give a popular basis to their self-interested claims. But while such claims are often manufactured, they can have a profound effect on "real" movements, or at least on how they are framed by the media. As parties have been hollowed out, both true movements and top-down, bottom-up hybrids have occupied much of the space that parties once monopolized.

But the expansion of movement-like mobilization to other kinds of groups is not the only important trend in the American political system. As the grip of parties and Congress has weakened, there has been a corresponding strengthening of the federal executive, reinforced by the creation of a strong administrative armature. From the New Deal onward, but especially during World War Two and the Cold War, the power of the executive has expanded, leaving the parties' bases and their national offices increasingly outside the circle of policymaking. As Jacobs, King, and Milkis wrote, "the dimension of conflict that divided Democrats and Republicans during the New Deal ... was displaced by a struggle for the resources and powers of the administrative state" (2019: 460).

An early sign of this trend came in the 1960s with the Johnson administration, and in the 1980s during the so-called "Reagan Revolution." "Only with Johnson," write Milkis and Tichenor, "was the full panoply of modern presidential powers – political, administrative, and rhetorical – deployed on behalf of insurgent interests and demands." At a time when Congress and the parties were becoming subordinate to the presidency, "Johnson claimed broad authority to transform domestic policy on his own terms" (2019:37). This was also the period in which the civil rights movement was effectively combining institutional "insider" with "outsider" collective action: "Consequently, Johnson and the civil rights movement formed a more direct, combustible, and transformative relationship that was true of previous collaborations between presidents and social movements" (2019:37).

The Reagan administration had a less hands-on relationship with the New Right than Johnson did with civil rights leaders. But by this time, the generation of leaders who had emerged from the Goldwater campaign was deeply embedded in the core of the GOP and Reagan had formed a partnership with Christian Right leaders that would endure into the new century. Although he continued to frame his administration as an antidote to the growth of the administrative state, "Reagan contributed significantly to the development of an executive-centered, nationalized party system that abetted rather than impeded centralized administration" (2019:37).

The theory of the "unitary executive" that appeared to guide the national security policies of the second Bush administration, and the aggressive personalization of the state by the Trump administration, were the ultimate outcome of the growth of partisan administration over the preceding decades. Rather than reducing the power of the central state, these Republican administrations "redeployed" it.

But how, analysts and pundits asked, could as ill-prepared and erratic a figure as Donald Trump have become the dominant actor in the Republican party, with its 150-year history of winning elections and holding together a diverse constituency? Scholars and publicists have proposed a variety of reasons for the Trumpian takeover of that party: the failure of the Republicans to come together around a viable insider candidate in 2016; Trump's rhetorical flair and jugular campaign skills (Mercieca 2020); the weakness of Hillary Clinton's campaign and the widespread hatred for her after thirty years of Republican denigration; and the failure of Barack Obama to put substantial resources into the Democratic party organization as he built his own movement organization (Milkis and York 2017).

In the developmental spirit of this Element, I take a longer view. First, as we have seen, the "hollowing out" of the party system began much earlier than these developments, leaving the Republicans easy prey to an assault from an outsider with a talent for exacerbating conflict. Second, the once-insurgent Tea Party activists constituted a populist/nationalist base within the party that Trump could amplify (Gervais and Morris 2018). Looking further back, the New Right and Christian conservatives who entered the party in the 1970s and 1980s had merged with mainstream economic conservatives who could never believe that Trump's populist antics would cancel out his plutocratic instincts (Pierson 2017). That they were correct was shown during his first year in power when he rewarded them with the largest and most disproportionate tax cut in American history.

All of these legacies of past critical junctures were contributing factors to the weakening of party organizations, the strengthening of executive partisanship, and the polarization of the electorate. And one thing more: the dangerous and unmediated pattern of executive aggrandizement in the presence of polarization and of a weakened party system places American democracy in danger. This is the longest-term interaction between movements and parties in recent American political development.

6 Movements, Parties, and Democracy

In 1918 a wave of social protest swept across Italy, triggered in part by that country's disastrous intervention in the First World War, in part by the economic after-effects of that war, and in part by an electoral reform that had expanded the electorate to many thousands of inexperienced new voters. Much of the agitation of those years came from the Left – angered at the repressive policies of the war years and inspired by the revolution that had swept the Russian Tsars from power only in the preceding year (Tarrow 2021, ch. 9).

To many on the left, such as the young Marxist Antonio Gramsci, it seemed that Italian peasants and workers could do what the Bolsheviks had done in Russia. To conservatives, in the wake of the occupation of the factories that marked the high point of the cycle, there was widespread fear that Gramsci's hope would become a reality.

As the protest wave from the left declined, another movement – Benito Mussolini's Fascist movement – arose from the reaction to the war and the recession that had followed, with the support of a motley coalition of army veterans, peasants, small town thugs, wealthy landholders, and nationalists. Mussolini adopted a combination of populist and right-wing ideas, appealing both to militarism and to disgust that Italy's war experience had led to only modest territorial gains. He employed a combination of violent and nonviolent tactics and a mastery of the media for which both the Left and mainstream political groups were unprepared. He was the country's – and probably the world's – original populist.

Mussolini never came close to winning an electoral majority, but he took advantage of the divisions in the party system and the country's weak political institutions to come to power in 1922. On the Left, the country was split between feuding Communists and Socialists; on the Right, conservatives and liberals were divided by the war; and in the Center, a new Catholic party – the Partito Popolare – rejected the policies of both Left and Right and sought the votes of recently enfranchised peasants. These blocs were also internally divided: the Left over what had happened in Russia and its prospects for the West; the Right over how to combat the threat of revolution; and the *popolari* between a progressive wing and those who were too wedded to the Vatican to make common cause with either bloc.

He also used his talent as a journalist to seduce a following with a mixture of truths, half-truths, and outright lies (de Felice 2005). The result was that although his Partito Nazionale Fascista never came close to winning an election, no effective coalition existed to contest his claims and he walked into power after staging a theatrical "March on Rome."[33]

To put this outcome in terms that will resonate with the American present: because the Italian party system was so internally fractured, neither the divided Left, nor the splintered Right, nor the uncertain *popolari* had an effective answer to a political crisis, thus allowing a political adventurer with a charismatic appeal to come to power with a program of national renewal. Mussolini is not known to have said "Only I can fix it," as Donald Trump did, but during his rallies, his followers were schooled to chant "*Mussolini ha sempre ragione* (Mussolini is always right)".

But on his own, Mussolini was unlikely to have succeeded in subverting Italy's weak democratic institutions. His followers were inexperienced, most Italians had no idea how he would govern as a leader, and the country was deeply polarized. What allowed him to seize and consolidate power were two factors: institutional and political. The institutional factor was the weakness of a constitution that gave the King the power to choose whomever he wanted for prime minister regardless of the votes he controlled; the political factor was the willingness of liberal and conservative groups and parties to support the ascent of the future dictator on the theory that exercising power would exhaust his resources and make enemies, failing to understand that his was a social and political movement and not a conventional party like the ones that had governed Italy for the preceding sixty years.

Of course, the United States in the second decade of the twenty-first century looks nothing like the Italy of a century ago. For one thing, Americans had two centuries of electoral experience to draw upon and a constitution that had been tailored to divide power; for another, in contrast to the fractured Italian economy of 1918–1922, the American one in 2016 was booming; and, for a third, there was no revolution afoot in the world to inspire some and terrorize others, as there had been in 1917. But the United States had been fighting an endless war and suffering increased inequality in the midst of plenty for almost two decades, helping to create a deeply polarized society in the presence of a weakened party system.

As in Italy a century ago, Americans were deeply divided. A populist left, under the leadership of a septagenarian senator from Vermont, struck out at

---

[33] To be more precise, the future *Duce* arrived in Rome in a sleeping car while his squads of fascist thugs marched on city halls around the country.

what it saw as a regime of raw capitalism; the moderate center-left had lost its charismatic leader, Barack Obama, who stepped down as president after the obligatory two terms, handing the party's reins to an unpopular female successor who lacked his charisma and his appeal to black Americans. As in Italy, institutions and politics combined to open the way for the ascendance of a demagogic outsider: The electoral system was marred by an electoral college that allowed a "strongman" (Ben-Ghiat 2020) who had gained a minority of the popular vote to come to power; and, just as Italian Liberals and Conservatives thought they could manage Mussolini, Republican elites thought they could control an inexperienced real estate operator and reality TV figure.

Not only that, the "Trumpian moment" was the result of a much longer movement that had prepared the ground for Trump's election and for his combination of populism and plutocracy (Pierson 2017). As Thomas Patterson writes, this was the culmination of a long process of Republican evolution:

> The GOP has walked itself into five traps, each of which threatens its future ... One trap is its steady movement to the right, which has distanced the party from the moderate voters who hold the balance of power in a two-party system. A second trap is demographic change ... Right-wing media are the Republicans' third trap ... A fourth trap is the large tax cuts that the GOP has three times given the wealthy ... The fifth trap is the GOP's disregard for democratic norms and institutions, including its effort through voter ID laws to suppress the vote of minorities and lower-income Americans. In the process, it has made lasting enemies and created instruments of power that can be used against it. (Patterson 2020:3–4)

Patterson's indictment of the GOP is sound as far as it goes, but it goes only as far as the boundaries of the party system. The Republican party has indeed moved steadily to the right; it has certainly narrowed its base to mostly older, majority male, and overwhelmingly white people; it has aligned itself with the most retrograde messengers in the mediascape; it has given tax cuts to the very rich while claiming to serve the interests of The People; and it has shown a chilling indifference to democratic norms and institutions. But those errors and transgressions have been triggered by the rise of a series of social movements and other groups that – rather than challenging the party from the outside – had become central to its ideological mission.

Looking backward, we can see that parties, movements, and democracy have intersected in the Republican party's history since its inception in 1854. Looking forward, it is hard to predict what will happen to the party and, by extension, to the two-party system, after Trump. Pundits have made many predictions: "Whither Trumpism?" asked one. "What will a post-Trump GOP look like?" asked another.

"Republicans prep for leadership battle if Trump goes down," said a third. "On the trail: the first signs of a post-Trump GOP," offered a fourth.[34]

If Trump was an ordinary politician, predicting what will happen to a party that wrapped itself in his coattails might be simpler. But Trump came to power as the leader of a *movement*, and everything he did as President can be interpreted as efforts to defend that buttress. Another way of putting this is that the ideological structuring of the Republican party dovetailed with the personalism of the leader to produce a series of crude policy initiatives that skirted – and often crossed – the line between the rule of law and its destruction.

Moreover, movements have a way of enduring even when their leaders disappear. Particularly given that the Trumpian movement had its basis in four decades of Republican party evolution and was built on the racial resentment that is still potent in many parts of White America, "it may be too late to put Trump back in the bottle," as Stuart Stevens argued in *It Was All a Lie* (2020). The perambulations of the Republican political elite after Trump's defeat in November 2020 show that it is no longer clear where that party will go or whether it will remain a unified party.

But what about democracy? Although the Republicans did not fight the Civil War in order to defend democracy, the outcome of that war was to broaden the democratic system by extending rights to the newly freed slaves – at least in theory. Favoring their northern and western constituents in the rest of the century was also not aimed at democracy, but at melding the interests of its electorate with a burgeoning capitalist system. As the turn of the century neared, the party was challenged by three insurgent groups: first farmers, then women, and finally the Progressives. Those were either explicitly or implicitly democracy-expanding movements, but African Americans were largely absent from all three. Expanding democracy would have to come from elsewhere.

Over the next half-century, and with occasional alliances, black Americans fought the strictures of Jim Crow, shifted to urban environments where they could develop civic and political skills, and created a civil rights movement with support from allies who helped them reclaim their rights in what Richard Vallely has called "The Second Reconstruction" (2004). In the wake of that movement, other minorities, women, and LGBTQ people adopted the same "formative" combination of approaches (Milkis and Tichenor 2019). Democratization has been slow, halting, and has suffered reverses, sometimes at the hands of the same Supreme Court that led the way from segregation in the 1950s.

---

[34] www.theguardian.com/us-news/2020/aug/08/trump-republican-party-future-election-trumpism?CMP=Share_iOSApp_Other.

If race is central to this story, it is because it has been the red thread of conflict alignment throughout American history – no less in the election of Donald Trump than in the Civil War and Reconstruction, the "Redemption" of the South by segregationist southerners, the largely white agrarians, the suffragists, and the Progressives. But race was also threaded through Woodrow Wilson's segregationist policies, FDR's indifference to black rights, the Dixiecrat revolt of 1948, and the countermovement of Klan violence and White Citizens' Councils following the *Brown* decision. It is not an exaggeration to say that race was one of the most incandescent components of almost every critical juncture since the Civil War.

It is no accident, therefore, that race was at the center of the critical juncture that began with Trump's election in 2016, proceeded as he and his administration whittled away at the administrative state and the rule of law, and peaked with the Coronavirus crisis, its economic aftershocks, and the election of 2020. Racial politics have been woven into the fabric of American democracy – and of *un*democracy – since the founding. It is therefore fitting that the latest critical juncture is imbricated with a mix of race, the demand for racial justice, and the beginning of what may turn out to be the first sustained movement that unites black, brown, and white Americans in a fight for democracy. If that turns out to be true, what a legacy that would be for George Floyd!

References

Aldrich, J. H. (1995). *Why Parties? The Origin and Transformation of Party Politics in America*. Chicago: University of Chicago Press.

Almeida, P. (2008). *Waves of Protest: Popular Struggle in El Salvador, 1925–2005*. Minneapolis: University of Minnesota Press.

Almeida, P. (2010). *Social Movement Partyism: Collective Action and Oppositional Political Parties*. Minneapolis and St. Paul: University of Minnesota Press.

Almond, G. A. and S. Verba (1964). *The Civic Culture: Political Attitudes and Democracy in Five Nations*. Princeton, NJ: Princeton University Press.

Amenta, E. (2005). "Political Contexts, Challenger Strategies, and Mobilization: Explaining the Impact of the Townsend Plan." In D. Meyer, V. Jenness, and H. Ingram, eds. *Routing the Opposition: Social Movements, Public Policy and Democracy*. Minneapolis: University of Minnesota Press, ch. 1.

Amenta, E. (2006). *When Movements Matter: The Townsend Plan and the Rise of Social Security*. Princeton, NJ: Princeton University Press.

Aminzade, R., J. Goldstone, D. McAdam, W. Sewell, S. Tarrow, and C. Tilly. (2021). *Silence and Voice in the Study of Contentious Politics*. Cambridge: Cambridge University Press.

Andrews, K. (2002). "Movement-Countermovement Dynamics and the Emergence of New Institutions: The Case of 'White Flight' Schools in Mississippi." *Social Forces* 80: 911–936.

Anria, S. (2019). *When Movements Become Parties: The Bolivian MAS in Comparative Perspective*. Cambridge and New York: Cambridge University Press.

Aytaç, S. E. and S. C. Stokes (2019). *Why Bother? Rethinking Participation in Elections and Protests*. New York and Cambridge: Cambridge University Press.

Bawn, K., M. Cohen, D. Karol, S. Masket, H. Noel, and J. Zaller. (2012). "A Theory of Political Parties: Groups, Policy Demands and Nominations in American Politics." *Perspectives on Politics* 10: 571–597.

Ben-Ghiat, R. (2020). *Strongmen: Mussolini to the Present*. New York: Norton.

Bensel, R. F. (1990). *Yankee Leviathan. The Origins of Central Authority in America, 1859–1877*. New York and Cambridge: Cambridge University Press.

Blings, S. (2020). "Niche Parties and Social Movements: Mechanisms of Programmatic Alignment and Party Success." *Government and Opposition* **55**: 220–240.

Blum, R. M. (2020). *How the Tea Party Captured the GOP: Insurgent Factions in American Politics*. Chicago: University of Chicago Press.

Boix, C., Ed. (2009). *Oxford Handbook of Comparative Politics*. Oxford and New York: Oxford University Press.

Bremer, B., S. Hutter and H. Kriesi. (2020a). "Dynamics of Protest and Electoral Politics in the Great Recession." *European Journal of Political Research* **59**: 1–25.

Bremer, B., S. Hutter, and H. Kriesi (2020b). "Electoral Punishment and Protest Politics in Times of Crisis." In H. Kriesi, J. Lorenzini, B. Wüest, and S. Hausermann, eds. *Contention in Times of Crisis: Recession and Political Protest in Thirty European Countries*. Cambridge and New York: Cambridge University Press, ch. 10.

Burnham, W. D. (1970). *Critical Elections and the Mainsprings of American Politics*. New York: W.W. Norton.

Campbell, A., P. Converse, W. Miller, and D. Stokes. (1960). *The American Voter*. New York: Wiley.

Cantrell, G. (2020). *The People's Revolt: Texas Populists and the Roots of American Liberalism*. New Haven, CT: Yale University Press.

Chen, A. (2020). "Black Lives Matter, CHS, and the Current Moment." *Trajectories* **31**: 23–38.

Cohen, M., D. Karol, H. Noel, and J. Zaller. (2008). *The Party Decides: Presidential Nominations Before and After Reform*. Chicago: University of Chicago Press.

Collier, D. and R. Collier (1991). *Shaping the Political Arena: Critical Junctures, the Labor Movement, and Regime Dynamics in Latin America*. Princeton: Princeton University Press.

Collier, D. and G. Munck, eds. (2017). *Symposium on Critical Junctures and Historical Legacies*. Qualitative and Multi-Method Research. Washington, DC: American Political Science Association.

Collier, D. and G. Munck (in press). *Critical Junctures and Historical Legacies: Insights and Tools for Comparative Social Science*. Lanham MD: Rowman and Littlefield.

de Felice, R. (2005). *Mussolini giornalista*. Milan: Rizzoli.

Della Porta, D., J. Fernandez, , H. Kourki, and L. Mosca (2017). *Movement Parties Against Austerity*. Cambridge: Polity.

Della Porta, D. and M. Diani (2006). *Social Movements: An Introduction*, 2nd edition. Malden, MA and Oxford: Blackwell Publishing.

Donoso, Sofia and Marisa von Bülow, eds. 2017. *Social Movements in Chile: Organization, Trajectories, and Political Consequences.* New York: Palgrave Macmillan.

Downs, A. (1957). *An Economic Theory of Democracy.* New York: Harper.

Du Bois, W. E. B. (1935). *Black Reconstruction in America: An Essay Toward a History of the Part Which Black Folk Played in the Attempt to Reconstruct Democracy in America, 1860–1880.* New York: Harcourt, Brace.

Dudziak, M. L. (2000). *Cold War Civil Rights.* Princeton: Princeton University Press.

Eisinger, P. (1973). "The Conditions of Protest Behavior in American Cities." *American Political Science Review* **67**:11–28.

Fisher, D. R. (2018). "Climate of Resistance: How the Climate Movement Connected to the Resstance." In David S. Meyer and Sidney Tarrow, eds., *The Resistance.* Oxford University Press, ch. 5.

Fisher, D. R. (2019). *American Resistance: From the Women's March to the Blue Wave.* New York: Columbia University Press.

Fisher, D. R. (2020). "The Diversity of the Recent Black Lives Matter Protests is a Good Sign for Racial Equity." *How We Rise.* Brookings Institution, 8 July.

Foner, E. (2014). *Reconstruction: America's Unfinished Revolution.* New York: Harper Perennial.

Francis, M. M. (2014). *Civil Rights and the Making of the Modern American State.* New York and Cambridge: Cambridge University Press.

Frymer, P. (1999). *Uneasy Alliances: Race and Party Competition in America.* Princeton: Princeton University Press.

Gamson, W. A. (1990). *The Strategy of Social Protest.* Belmont, CA: Wadsworth Pub. Co.

Gervais, B. and I. Morris (2018). *Reactionary Republicanism: How the Tea Party Paved the Way for Trump's Victory.* New York and Oxford: Oxford University Press.

Gillion, D. Q. (2020). *The Loud Minority: Why Protests Matter in American Democracy.* Princeton: Princeton University Press.

Giugni, M. and S. Yamasaki (2009). "The Policy Impact of Social Movements: A Replication through Qualitative Comparative Analysis." *Mobilization* **14**: 467–484.

Giugni, M., D. McAdam, and C. Tilly (1999a). *From Contention to Democracy.* Lanham, MD: Rowman and Littlefield.

Giugni, M., D. Mc Adam, and C. Tilly (1999b). *How Social Movements Matter.* Minneapolis: University of Minnesota Press.

Goldstone, J. A., ed. (2003). *State, Parties, and Social Movements.* New York and Cambridge: Cambridge University Press.

Grossmann, M. and D. Hopkins (2016). *Asymmetric Politics: Ideological Republicans and Group Interest Democrats.* New York: Oxford University Press.

Hans Noel. 2012. "Which Long Coalition? The Creation of the Anti–slavery Coalition." *Party Politics* 19: 962–984.

Heaney, M. T. and F. Rojas (2015). *Party in the Street: The Antiwar Movement and the Democratic Party After 9/11.* New York: Cambridge University Press.

Hunter, W. (2011). *The Transformation of the Workers' Party of Brazil, 1989– 2009.* New York and Cambridge: Cambridge University Press.

Hutter, S. (2014). "Protest Event Analysis and its Offspring." In D. della Porta, ed., *Methodological Practices in Social Movement Research.* Oxford: Oxford University Press, ch. 14.

Jacobs, N. F., D. King and S. M. Milkis (2019). "Building a Conservative State: Partisan Polarization and the Redeployment of Administrative Power." *Perspectives on Politics* 17: 453–469.

Jacobs, N. F. and S. M. Milkis (2022). *What Happened to the Vital Center.* Oxford: Oxford Univerity Press.

Katz, R. S. and P. Mair (1993). "The Evolution of Party Organizations in Europe: The Three Faces of Party Organization." *American Review of Politics* 14: 593–618.

Katznelson, I. (2013). *Fear Itself: The New Deal and the Origins of Our Time.* New York: Liveright.

Keck, M. (1992). *The Worker's Party and Democratization in Brazil.* New Havan and London: Yale University Press.

Key, V. O. (1955). "A Theory of Critical Elections." *Journal of Politics* 17: 3–18.

Key, V. O. (1984). *Southern Politics in State and Nation.* Knoxville, TX: University of Tennessee Press.

Kitschelt, H. (1986). "Political Opportunity Structures and Political Protest: Anti-Nuclear Movements in Four Democracies." *British Journal of Political Science* 16: 57–85.

Kitschelt, H. (2006). "Movement Parties." In R. A. Katz and B. Krotty, eds., *Handbook of Party Politics.*London: Sage Publications, ch. 24.

Klandermans, B. (2018). "How Citizens Try to Influence Politics: On Movements and Parties." Unpublished paper presented to the Closing Conference of the PolPart project, Amsterdam.

Kolb, F. (2007). *Protest and Opportunities: The Political Outcomes of Social Movements.* Frankfurt and New York: Campus.

Kriesi, H. (1995). The Political Opportunity Structure of the New Social Movements: Its Impact on Their Mobilization. *The Politics of Social Protest.* J. C. Jenkins and B. Klandermans. Minneapolis and St. Paul: University of Minnesota Press, ch. 7

Kriesi, H., S. Hutter, and A. Bojar (2019). "Contentious Episode Analysis." *Mobilization* **29**: 1–26.

Kriesi, H., R. Koopmans, J. W. Duyvendak, and M. Giugni. (1995). *The Politics of New Social Movements in Western Europe.* Minneapolis and St. Paul: University of Minnesota Press.

Kriesi, H., J. Lorenzini, B. Wüest, and S. Hausermann. (2020). *Contention in Times of Crisis. Comparing Political Protest in 30 European Countries, 2000–2015.* Cambridge: Cambridge University Press.

Lieberman, R. C., S. Mettler, and. K. M. Roberts, eds. (2021). *Democratic Resilience: Can the United States Withstand Rising Polarization?* New York, Cambridge University Press.

Lipset, S. M. and S. Rokkan (1967). *Party Systems and Voter Alignments: Cross-national Perspectives.* Glencoe, IL: Free Press.

Luders, J. E. (2003). "Countermovements, the State, and the Intensity of Racial Contention in the American South." In J. A. Goldstone, ed., *States, Parties and Social Movements.* New York and Cambridge: Cambridge University Press, ch. 1.

Luna, J. P. and D. Altman (2011). "Uprooted but Stable: Chilean Parties and the Concept of Party System Institutionalization." *Latin American Politics and Society* **53**: 1–28.

Mahoney, J. (2000). "Path Dependence in Historical Sociology." *Theory and Society* **24**: 507–548.

Mayer N. Zald and John McCarthy, eds. (1987). *Social Movements in an Organizational Society: Collected Essays.* Piscataway, NJ: Transaction Press.

Mayhew, D. (1986). *Placing Parties in American Politics: Organization, Electoral Settings, and Government Activity.* Princeton, NJ: Princeton University Press.

McAdam, D. (1999a). "The Biographical Impact of Activism." In M. Giuni, D. McAdam and C. Tilly, eds., *How Social Movements Matter.* Minneapolis and St. Paul: University of Minnesota, ch. 6.

McAdam, D. (1999b). *Political Process and the Development of Black Insurgency, 1930–1970.* Chicago: University of Chicago Press.

McAdam, D. (2020). "We've Never Seen Protests Like These Before." *Jacobin.* January, 6. www.jacobinmag.com/2020/06/george-floyd-protests-black-lives-matter-riots-demonstrations

McAdam, D. and K. Kloos (2014). *Deeply Divided: Racial Politics and Social Movements in Post-War America.* New York: Oxford University Press.

McAdam, D. and S. Tarrow (2010). "Ballots and Barricades: The Reciprocal Relations Between Elections and Social Movements." *Perspectives on Politics* **8**: 529–542.

McAdam, D., S. Tarrow, and C. Tilly. (2001). *Dynamics of Contention*. New York and Cambridge, Cambridge University Press.

McCarthy, J. and M. N. Zald (1977). "Resource Mobilization and Social Movements: A Partial Theory." *American Journal of Sociology* **82**: 1212–1241.

McCarty, N. and E. Schickler (2018). "On The Theory of Parties." *Annual Review of Political Science* **21**: 175–193.

Melucci, A. (1980). "The New Social Movements: A Theoretical Approach." *Social Science Information* **19**: 199–226.

Mercieca, J. (2020). *Demagogue for President: The Rhetorical Genius of Donald Trump*. College Station TX: Texas A & M University Press.

Mettler, S. and R. Lieberman (2020). *Four Threats: The Recurring Crises of American Democracy*. New York: Palgrave Macmillan.

Meyer, D. S. and S. Staggenborg (1996). "Movements, Countermovements, and the Structure of Political Opportunity." *American Journal of Sociology* **101**: 1628–1660.

Meyer, D. S. and S. Tarrow (1998). *The Social Movement Society: Contentious Politics for a New Century*. Lanham, MD: Rowman and Littlefield.

Meyer, D. S. and S. Tarrow, eds. (2018). *The Resistance: The Dawn of the Anti-Trump Opposition Movement*. Oxford: Oxford University Press.

Milkis, S. M. (1993). *The President and the Parties: The Transformation of the American Party System Since the New Deal*. New York and Oxford: Oxford University Press.

Milkis, S. M. and D. J. Tichenor (2019). *Rivalry and Reform: Presidents, Social Movements, and the Transformation of American Politics*. Chicago: University of Chicago Press.

Milkis, s. M. and D.J. Tichenor 2021). "When Revolutions Go Backward: Democratic Precarity in American Political Development," unpublished paper.

Milkis, S. M. and J. W. York (2017). "Barack Obama, Organizing for Action, and Executive-Centered Partisanship." *Studies in American Political Development* **31**: 1–23.

Minkoff, D. C. (1995). *Organizing for Equality: The Evolution of Women's and Racial-ethnic Organizations in America, 1955–1985*. New Brunswick, NJ: Rutgers University Press.

Mudde, C. and C. R. Kaltwasser, Eds. (2012). *Populism in Europe and the Americas: Threat or Corrective for Democracy?* Cambridge: Cambridge University Press.

Munck, G. (in preparation). "When Causes are Distant and Effects Persist: Rethinking the Critical Juncture Framework." In D.Collier and G.Munck, eds., *Critical Junctures and Historical Legacies: Insights and Tools for Comparative Social Science*. Lanham, MD: Romwan and Littlefield, ch.2.

Noel, H. (2014). *Political Ideologies and Political Parties in America.* New York: Cambridge University Press.

Offe, C. (1985). "New Social Movements: Challenging the Boundaries of Institutional Politics." *Social Research* **52**: 817–868.

Parker, C. S. and M. A. Barreto (2013). *Change They Can't Believe In: The Tea Party and Reactionary Politics in America.* Princeton, NJ: Princeton University Press.

Patterson, T. E. (2020). *Is the Republican Party Destroying Itself?* Seattle, WA: KDP Publishing.

Perlstein, R. (2009). *Before the Storm: Barry Goldwater and the Unmaking of the American Consensus.* New York: Nation Books.

Perlstein, R. (2020). *Reaganland: America's Right Turn, 1976–1980.* New York: Simon and Schuster.

Pierson, P. (2017). "American Hybrid: Donald Trump and the Strange Merger of Populism and Plutocracy." *British Journal of Sociology* **68**: S10–S119.

Piven, F. F. and R. Cloward (1972). *Regulating the Poor.* New York: Vintage Books.

Piven, F. F. and R. Cloward (1977). *Poor People's Movements: Why They Succeed, How They Fail.* New York: Vintage.

Roberts, K. (2015). *Changing Course in Latin America: Party Systems in the Neoliberal Era.* New York and Cambridge: Cambridge University Press.

Rosenfeld, S. (2018). *The Polarizers: Postwar Architects of our Partisan Era.* Chicago, IL: University of Chicago Press.

Rucht, D. and T. Ohlemacher (1992). "Protest Event Data: Collection, Uses and Perspectives." In M. Diani and R. Eyerman, eds., *Studying Collective Action.* London, Sage Publications, pp. 76–106.

Schickler, E. (2016). *Racial Realignment: The Transformation of American Liberalism, 1932–1965.* Princeton, NJ: Princeton University Press.

Schlozman, D. (2015). *When Movements Anchor Parties: Electoral Alignments in American History.* Princeton and Oxford: Princeton University Press.

Schlozman, D. and S. Rosenfeld (2018). The Long New Right and the World it Made. Presented to the annual conference of the American Political Science Association. Boston, MA.

Schlozman, D. and S. Rosenfeld (2019). "The Hollow Parties." In F. Lee and N. McCarty, eds., *Can America Govern Itself?* New York and Cambridge, Cambridge University Press, ch. 6.

Shafer, B. E. (1983). *The Struggle for the Democratic Party and the Shaping of Post-Reform Politics.* New York: Russell Sage Foundation.

Skocpol, T. and A. Hertel-Fernandez (2016a). "The Koch Effect." *Inequality Mini-Conference of the Souther Political Science Association.* San Juan, Puerto Rico.

Skocpol, T. and A. Hertel-Fernandez (2016b). "The Koch Network and Republican Party Extremism." *Perspectives on Politics* **14**: 681–699.

Skocpol, T. and C. Tervo, Eds. (2020). *Upending American Politics: Polarizing Parties, Ideological Elites, and Citizen Activists from the Tea Party to the Anti-Trump Resistance.* New York: Oxford University Press.

Skocpol, T. and V. Williamson (2011). *The Tea Party and the Remaking of Republican Conservatism.* New York and Oxford: Oxford University Press.

Snow, D.,. A. Soule, and H. Kriesi, Eds. (2004). *Blackwell Companion to Social Movements.* London: Wiley-Blackwell.

Snow, D., S. A. Soule, and H. Kriesi, Eds. (2018). *Blackwell Companion to Social Movements.* London: Wiley-Blackwell.

Stevens, S. (2020). *It Was All a Lie: How the Republican Party Became Donald Trump.* New York: Penguin Random House.

Tarrow, S. (1990). "The Phantom at the Opera: Political Parties and Social Movements in Italy in the 1960s and 1970s." In R. Dalton and M. Kuechler, eds., *Challenging the Political Order.* New Haven: Yale University Press, pp. 251–273.

Tarrow, S. (2018). "Rhythms of Resistance: The Anti-Trumpian Moment in a Cycle of Contention."S In D. S. Meyer and S. Tarrow, eds., *The Resistance: The Dawn of the Anti-Trump Opposition Movement.* New York: Oxford University Press, pp. 187–206.

Tarrow, S. (2021). *Movements and Parties in American Political Develpment.* New York and Cambridge, Cambridge University Press.

Teele, D. L. (2018a). *Forging the Franchise: The Political Origins of the Women's Vote.* Princeton NJ, Princeton University Press.

Teele, D. L. (2018b). "How the West Was Won: Competition, Mobilization, and Women's Enfranchisement in the United States." *Journal of Politics* **80**: 442–461.

Tichenor, D. and R. Harris (2003). "Organized Interests and American Political Development." *Political Science Quarterly* **117**: 587–612.

Tilly, C. (1978). *From Mobilization to Revolution.* Reading: Addison-Wesley.

Tilly, C. (1983). "Speaking Your Mind without Elections, Surveys, or Social Movements." *Public Opinion Quarterly* **47**: 461–478.

Tilly, C. (1990). *Coercion, Capital, and European States, AD 990–1992.* Cambridge, MA: Blackwell.

Tilly, C. (1995). *Popular Contention in Great Britain, 1758–1834.* Cambridge, MA: Harvard University Press.

Tilly, C. (2006). *Regimes and Repertoires.* Cambridge: Cambridge University Press.

Tilly, C. and S. Tarrow (2015). *Contentious Politics, 2nd ed.* New York: Oxford University Press.

Touraine, A. (1971). *The May Movement: Revolt and Reform.* New York: Random House.

Truman, D. (1951). *The Governmental Process*. New York: Knopf.

Vallely, R. M. (2004). *The Two Reconstructions: The Struggle for Black Enfranchisement*. Chicago, IL: University of Chicago Press.

Vallely, R., S. Mettler, and R. Lieberman, eds. (2016). *Oxford Handbook of American Political Development*. Oxford: Oxford University Press.

Walker, E. (2014). *Grassroots for Hire: Public Affairs Consultants in American Democracy*. New York: Cambridge University Press.

Cambridge Elements ☰

Contentious Politics

David S. Meyer
University of California, Irvine

David S. Meyer is Professor of Sociology and Political Science at the University of California, Irvine. He has written extensively on social movements and public policy, mostly in the United States, and is a winner of the John D. McCarthy Award for Lifetime Achievement in the Scholarship of Social Movements and Collective Behavior.

Suzanne Staggenborg
University of Pittsburgh

Suzanne Staggenborg is Professor of Sociology at the University of Pittsburgh. She has studied organizational and political dynamics in a variety of social movements, including the women's movement and the environmental movement, and is a winner of the John D. McCarthy Award for Lifetime Achievement in the Scholarship of Social Movements and Collective Behavior.

About the series

Cambridge Elements series in Contentious Politics provides an important opportunity to bridge research and communication about the politics of protest across disciplines and between the academy and a broader public. Our focus is on political engagement, disruption, and collective action that extends beyond the boundaries of conventional institutional politics. Social movements, revolutionary campaigns, organized reform efforts, and more or less spontaneous uprisings are the important and interesting developments that animate contemporary politics; we welcome studies and analyses that promote better understanding and dialogue.

Cambridge Elements ☰

Contentious Politics

Elements in the Series

The Phantom at The Opera: Social Movements and Institutional Politics
Sidney Tarrow

A full series listing is available at: www.cambridge.org/ECTP

Printed in the United States
by Baker & Taylor Publisher Services